THE COMPLETE BERNESE MOUNTAIN DOG

JUDE SIMONDS

RINGPRESS

Acknowledgements

Special thanks to Ernst Schlucter, Wolfgang and Rosika Hermes, Maggie Davis, Gillian Sharman and Brenda Griffiths for loaning many of their treasured photographs; and to everyone else who sent photos for possible inclusion.

To Brian, my husband, for his total commitment to our hobby; Vreni Gasser, her devotion to the Bernese Mountain Dog has been my inspiration, and to Eric Taylor, Robert Lees and Jenny Smith who give so much of themselves so willingly and who have taught me so much.

Published by Ringpress Books 1989
Spirella House, Bridge Road, Letchworth, Herts SG6 4ET

© 1989 Jude Simonds

Production Consultants: Landmark Ltd of London
Typeset by Area Graphics Ltd., Letchworth, Herts
Printed and bound in Great Britain by The Bath Press

ISBN 0 948955 651

Contents

Durrbachler: The colouring and markings varied greatly from today's Bernese.

Beringer and Pampaluchi

CHAPTER ONE

The Origins Of The Bernese Mountain Dog

FROM early writings, the theory that the Bernese Mountain Dog is a descendant of the ancient Mollossus dogs of Roman times has been accepted by many without question. The German writer Strebel included this theory in his book *The German Dogs*, and the idea was continued by Professor Heim, without questioning. Heim's booklet published in 1914 was the main source of information over the next fifty years, and its theories were copied by others. Recent excavations have unearthed the skulls of large dogs which could be the forebears of Bernese, and these date from the Bronze and Iron ages. It can be assumed from these recovered remains that the Celts, who were keepers of cattle, already had large, strong dogs for protection of both stock and property. There is no apparent reason why the Romans would have imported the Mollossus to do the same job when adequate dogs could be found locally, although there is no way of knowing if Mollossus blood was introduced into the existing breeds.

There is no proof or indication that the breed, in recognisable form, goes back very far in year terms. It appears that it is only from about AD1000 that dogs of a distinct type were bred in any particular area. Types of dog needed for hunting and herding would have been carefully developed, but a watch dog could be any shape or size or colour. It is noted that at around AD1000, the settlers in the Swiss country areas were able to have a settled existence with little outside influence to cause disruption. It is thought that the farmers were reasonably well off, and so they were more able to keep large dogs, whereas in other areas poverty prevented people from keeping large dogs. Small dogs have always had a good following, as indeed they do now.

In 1523 Conrad Gessner wrote: *"Some of the big and strong dogs are especially trained to stay around the houses and stables and in the fields. They must protect the cattle from danger. Some guard the cattle, some the fields and some the houses. Other dogs are trained to protect people. They must contend after murderers and other mean people. They must be fierce and big and strong, as they must fight against warriors in their armour."*

Translation from the original may vary the occasional word, but there is no doubt here that selective breeding was being practised to produce farm dogs useful for varying tasks. Bernese Mountain Dogs developed from the farm dogs kept in the Berne Mittel land. Apart from giving warning and protecting the farm from thieves and wolves and bears which still roamed the countryside, it is apparent that some of these large farm dogs were used as drovers. Herdsmen would have preferred smaller, more agile dogs for this purpose as have been developed throughout the world, but there is no doubt that larger dogs were used for this task. Even though selective breeding was being practised, there was much inter-breeding between the various types of dog. From about 1850, cheeseries were being built in the valleys and in the mittel lands, and the farmers started to use the dogs to haul the milk to these cheeseries by harnessing them to small carts. It was usually the job of the smallest boy in the family to accompany the dog, so the stability of the dog's temperament would have been important.

Around the same period, there was much more awareness of the different types of dog and foreign breeds were continually gaining popularity. The St Bernard, with his massive size and red or yellow and white colouring, became very fashionable, and the Bernese farm dogs became less common. These Bernese farmers' dogs were of no standard colour, and there is no evidence to suggest that selection for colour was extensively practised; size and character were more important to the farmers. Some were black, white and tan in a recognisable pattern as we now know it, but many were solid red or a paler yellow colour, as well as either of these colours marked with white. Studies of old paintings show dogs which could easily be Bernese as we know them today, but there are many colour combinations. Thousands of these yellow or red and white dogs were sold as St Bernards after 1850, and it is certain that many were no such thing. Tri-coloured dogs became less popular, and eventually only remote areas contained any number of these dogs. The people of Schwarzenburg were very poor, and there was little communication as the roads were bad and a train did not exist. Here the large tri-coloured dog retained its popularity, and so the type continued. Many craftsmen and farmers were too poor to own a horse, and so these large farm dogs were now commonly used as draught dogs, pulling the carts for weavers, butchers, dairymen and toolmakers. The influence of the new breeds was spreading, but there was a continued interest in the tri-coloured dogs in the rural areas south of Berne.

Before this time, there had been no breed name as such. They were known as butchers' dogs, farm dogs or cheesery dogs, and the markings and colour of the dogs also brought about a common name. Those dogs with a white ring around the neck in the form of a collar were called Ringgi, those with a definite white blaze on the face were called Blassi and dogs with little or no white on the face were called Bari which means 'little bear'. They were also known as the Gelbackler, which means 'yellow cheeks', and also the Vieraugli, four eyes, because of the tan markings over the eyes. The usefulness of these dogs was without question, and so a trade for buying and selling them developed as they continued to be used to bring produce into Berne from the outlying areas. An inn called the Durrbach Gasthaus became the centre of trade for these dogs.

PRESERVATION AND IMPROVEMENT OF THE BREED
The Swiss Kennel Club emerged in 1883, but the farmers' dogs were not recognised as a pure-bred type of dog. At the first show held, the Swiss hounds and the popular St Bernard were exhibited, but there were no mountain or farm dogs. Kennel Clubs had been formed in other countries, some more prosperous than Switzerland, and soon the Swiss

dog fanciers realised that high prices could be charged for St Bernards as interest abroad brought about many orders for puppies and adults. Many people pursued the furtherance of these new breeds, but there was also an interest in the old-fashioned type of dogs.

Franz Schertenleib was instrumental in bringing the tri-coloured farm dogs to a new popularity. An inn-keeper from Burgdorf, he had an interest in many forms of livestock and was fascinated by his father's stories of a distinctive type of farmer's dog. After some careful research, he went to the Durrbach region and bought one of these Durrbach dogs in 1892. Another theory that Schertenleib just happened upon one of these dogs has been put forward, but I suppose that this is one of those imponderable questions we shall never really know the answer to. We do know that Schertenleib became fanatical about the breed and searched throughout the canton of Berne for good specimens of Durrbachlers to add to his collection. It seems that Schertenleib was not concerned with monetary gain, but was genuine in his quest for preserving the breed. His enthusiasm seemed to be infectious, and other fanciers were soon attracted to the idea of preserving these dogs.

In 1899 Probst, another inn-keeper from Berne, wrote about these Durrbachlers in the Centralblatt newspaper. In 1904, Probst and a photographer friend, Doppler, organised a class at the Swiss Kennel Club International show at Berne where six dogs and one bitch were entered. Four of these went on to be registered by the Swiss Kennel Club in 1905. Dogs of unknown parentage were allowed entry into the Swiss Stud Book over the next ten years, if they received the approval of one of three experts on the breed. This task fell upon Schertenleib, his friend Dr Scheidegger, a Langenthal veterinary surgeon, and Gottfried Mumenthaler, a factory-owner and experienced dog-breeder. Max Schafroth, a weaver who owned a textile factory in Burgdorf, became involved in the breed at about the same time. He bought a dog and a bitch, and his enthusiasm helped the breed. These men were keen to work together in an effort to stabilise breed type and markings.

Mumenthaler became the owner of a bitch called Belline, parentage unknown, and this bitch was generally considered of exceptional quality and proved to be a great asset to the breed. Mumenthaler was a member of the Swiss Kennel Club and his experience was of great help to those early enthusiasts. But it was the Professor of Geology, Albert Heim, who became known as the father of the breed. One of the first members of the Swiss Kennel Club, he bred Newfoundlands but had a great interest in all breeds, especially working dogs. The interest shown in these old farm dogs attracted his attention, and the breed was certainly the richer for it. He made an extensive study of the four Swiss Mountain breeds, and it was in recognition of his work with Swiss dogs that the Albert Heim Foundation was started. Members of the Swiss Kennel Club, together with the director of the Natural History Museum, wanted to be sure that there would always be a centre for information about these dogs, and today the foundation is as popular as ever.

Meanwhile, the first fanciers had organised themselves into a breed club, and this was called Schweizerischer Durrbach Klub. Mumenthaler was president, with a full complement of ten committee members. Professor Heim thought that all these Swiss tri-colour dogs should be known under one collective name and suggested that the Durrbach dogs should become known as Berner Sennenhund. Members of the club did not agree with the change of name, especially as Heim did not live in the area and so only had involvement with the dogs at shows. These early breeders were right to oppose the proposal. The Senn is the name for the cattle herdsmen in the Alps, and smaller, more agile dogs were generally kept for their purposes. In fact, all the known Durrbach dogs had come from the lowlands, so the name did not seem appropriate at all. The literal translation of the suggested name is Bernese Alpine Herdsman's Dog. After a while, however, Heim persuaded the club members to change the name, arguing that the breed had originally been used throughout the canton of Berne and not just in the small Durrbach region where the dogs had remained while other breeds had increased in popularity. So a year after the club was started, Heim's suggestion was accepted and the Berner Sennenhund Klub came into being.

The interest in showing these dogs increased and in 1908 there were twenty-one exhibits at a show in Langenthal, and in 1910 an entry of forty-two was seen at a show in Berne. During the same year three dogs and five bitches were shown in Lausanne under the French classification of Bouvier Suisse. Throughout the world different names were given to this same breed. Today, in France and the French part of Switzerland, the breed is called Bouvier Bernois, and of course the American fanciers followed the British example in using Bernese Mountain Dog. The biggest event in the history of the breed was the club show held in Burgdorf on April 24, 1910. A total of one hundred and seven Bernese were entered, attracted no doubt by the free entry and the prizes on offer. Owners had been encouraged to bring their dogs so that a true picture of the breed could be obtained. I cannot help wondering how, if the breed had been so rare just five years earlier, there could have been so many Bernese in existence. Certainly, many of these dogs had great variations in markings from that which had become so desired – the true tri-colour. In those early litters there appeared yellow puppies, brown puppies, and even some without any white at all. Flecked, or brindled puppies were also common, which is not surprising when we consider the mixed background of some dogs.

The judge at this show in Burgdorf was Professor Heim, and while being encouraging to those who had come, he was not afraid to be critical of the dogs. A total of ninety-nine of the dogs entered had curly coats, the other eight had short hair. Eight dogs were disqualified as being untypical of the breed. A great number of the dogs were of unknown ancestry, but were accepted into the breed on their type. Heim told the breeders that the curly coats must be bred out, as he thought that they were not practical. Not all Bernese had the tan markings as seen in today's dogs, but Heim also wrote that the black head colour should never be over-shadowed by too much tan. There were black and tan dogs as well as those with a brown or yellow background colour. The preferred markings set out in 1910 were: white head markings, white on the nape of the neck, white ring around the neck, white on the chest, feet and tail tip.

Badly angulated dogs were commonplace, and this meant that many of these early dogs moved rather stiffly. Hind feet nearly always turned outwards, and the double hind dew-claw appeared on many dogs and bitches. Curled tails were seen often, but by far the most ugly fault was the split nose which was sometimes accompanied by a cleft palate

Bernese Mountain Dog/Bernese Cowherd's Dog. (Note third eyelids).

Beringer and Pampaluchi

deformity. Many of the dogs found in the Gurnigel area had this defect, whereby the nose is separated into two halves; the jaw is often deformed because of this causing the teeth to show all the time. As most of these dogs were also rather aggressive, some breeders felt that this trait should be preserved as the horrific appearance enhanced the aggressive behaviour. Heim convinced breeders that this defect should be eliminated, and only one of the exhibits at the 1910 show had this deformity. Of course, it did not disappear straightaway, but dogs like this were no longer shown and so were not in demand for breeding.

Superstitions abounded in remote farming areas, and there were still some people who wanted their Bernese to look fierce. Dogs with black feet and the double-dew claws were thought to have the power to keep evil spirits away, and light-coloured eyes coupled with dark faces added to the ferocious appearance. The blue eyes which sometimes occurred were even prized, although Heim continued to advise breeders that less fierce dogs should be bred, and a more friendly-looking type of dog was to be encouraged. This may explain why the wider white face markings soon became more sought after as the breed was kept for show purposes as well as for working.

From critiques, it appears that there were still great variations in size and body shape and these variations continued for some time. Sturdiness was, and still is, a trait to be encouraged, but it is not always easy to retain this aspect of the breed. In today's world, dog breeds have changed shape dramatically from the first specimens seen. Soundness and continuity of type must be a priority, but there is a tendency to change dogs to the stage where they lose their ability to fulfil their original function. The early farmers' dogs were kept in remote regions, as the dogs were useful and fulfilled a function. It therefore follows that although some characteristics of individual dogs needed to be bred out, we should sympathise with those breeders who wanted to retain the original characteristics. There is no doubt that the Bernese of today is a wonderful dog, but I wonder what the future would have held for these original farm dogs if they had not attracted the attention of Schertenleib, Heim and the others?

STABILISING CONFORMATION AND TYPE

Interest in shows continued and in 1911 they were held far and wide. Heim was still the most respected judge, and he was delighted to see the breed becoming more uniform with many good dogs, not just the exception. The farmers that took their dogs to shows had great pride in their animals, even though events did not always go according to plan. It is documented that one bitch was taken to a show and actually gave birth to puppies there! The breed club now boasted forty members and so it seemed that the breed was progressing well and not too quickly. The early enthusiasts were always keen to emphasise the fact that the dogs were bred to be useful, and the need to retain some characteristics was voiced over and over again. The dogs had to be of impressive appearance and proportions. They had to be strong enough to protect property and livestock, if necessary, and to come to their owner's aid in an emergency. But these dogs had to be trustworthy in normal situations and content to stay around the farm and not wander off.

In 1914, the majority of the dogs which were shown were Blassis; the Baris and Ringgis were becoming increasingly rare. Heim had written in 1910 that he liked to see the white markings, but they are not a necessary requirement of the breed. The popularity of Blassis continued, however, even to the extent that today far too much white is prized and purposely sought by some breeders. Heim also recorded the height of the Bernese that he judged, and the enormous variation of 50 to 73 cm (19½ to 27½ inches) was documented. Dogs without clear ancestry were still common, but good specimens were admitted to the Swiss Stud Book and so the start of pure breeding came about. Several breeders were breeding dogs of a definite family type and likeness, including the kennels of Dr Scheidegger (v Oberaargau), Schertenleib (v Schlossgut) and Mumenthaler (v Burigut).

In 1917, the Bernese had increased in popularity to such an extent that for the first time there were more registrations than for the Appenzellers, and by 1939 the Bernese had overtaken the St Bernard in popularity. Today, the Bernese is by far the most popular of all the Swiss breeds. Since the first Durrbachlers had been sought in 1882, and the formation of the breed club in 1907, the breed had undergone changes, but stability was being gained. The breed standard in 1936 was as follows:

Netty von Burgdorf, 12-9-1906, bred by Max Schafroth.

Illustration dated 1914 by Professor Albert Heim

General Appearance: A well-balanced dog, active and alert; a combination of sagacity, fidelity and utility.

Height: Dog 23 ins to 27½ ins; bitches 21 ins to 26 ins at shoulder.

Head: Skull flat, defined stop and strong muzzle. Dewlaps very slightly developed, flews not too pendulous, jaw strong with good, strong teeth. Eyes dark hazel-brown, full of fire. Ears V-shaped, set on high, not too pointed at tips and rather short. When in repose, hanging close to head; when alert, brought slightly forward and raised at base.

Body: Rather short than too long in back, compact and well ribbed up. Chest broad with good depth of brisket. Loins strong and muscular.

Legs and Feet: Forelegs perfectly straight and muscular, thighs well developed and stifles well bent. Feet round and compact. Dewclaws should be removed.

Tail: Of fair thickness and well covered with long hair, but not to form a flag; moderate length. When in repose, should be carried low, upward swirl permissible; when alert, may be carried gaily, but may never curl or be carried over back.

Coat: Soft and silky with bright, natural sheen; long and slightly wavy but may never curl.

Colour and Markings: Jet-black with russet-brown or deep tan markings on all four legs, a spot just above forelegs, each side of white chest markings and spots over eyes, which may never be missing. The brown on the forelegs must always be between the black and white.

Preferable, but not a condition, are: White feet, tip of tail, pure white blaze up foreface, a few white hairs on back of neck, and white star-shaped markings on chest. When the latter markings are missing, it is *not* a disqualification.

Faults: Too massive in head, light or staring eyes, too heavy or long ears, too narrow or snipy muzzle, under or overshot mouth, pendulous dewlaps, too long or Setter-like body, splay or hare feet, tail curled or carried over back, cow-hocks and white legs.

THE INTRODUCTION OF NEWFOUNDLAND BLOOD

Although dogs of unknown ancestry were used for breeding for many years, the loss of ancestry was small by the mid-1940s. In Basle at the dog show of 1947, there were five generations of Bernese on show. A living testimony of the pedigree, only the loss of seven Bernese from the sixth generation of sixty-four showed that in-breeding was rarely practised. The varied background of some dogs meant that the breed had a varied gene pool to draw upon, but discussions about the introduction of new blood became more frequent. The temperament of many Bernese left a lot to be desired: shyness was a particular problem. Club officials and members started to look around and investigate which breed would be the most suitable to introduce into the gene pool, but in 1948 an event occurred which was to put these ideas into the background. Following this incident, there has been much discussion as to whether a real accident or whether a planned experiment had taken place. The secretary subsequently tried to take credit for a planned experiment which had the support of the breed club, but we may never know exactly what led up to the event, although we do know what the outcome was.

A Bernese bitch called Christine v Lux was mated by the Newfoundland dog Pluto v

Erlengut when he jumped a fence into her kennel. Christine whelped three bitches and four dogs on December 21, 1948. All the puppies looked like Newfoundlands with a small amount of white on the feet. One bitch and three of the dogs were reared, but only the bitch was used for breeding. The breeder of this litter was an architect named Herr Bosiger, and he gave the bitch, called Babette, to the breed club, where she was passed on to Dr Hauser's care. She developed the conformation and the temperament of the Newfoundland, and in January 1951 she was mated to the Bernese Aldo v Tieffurt. On March 23, 1951 she whelped six live puppies and two dead. The dog and bitch born dead had white blazes; two dogs were black with white feet, white on the chin and a little white on the chest; one dog and one bitch were clearly Bernese but without the white blaze, and one dog and one bitch had Bernese markings except for a lack of white on the hind feet of the dog. Only the Bernese bitch, later named Christine v Schwarzwasserbachli, was reared by the president of the breed club, Herr Mischler.

At about nine-months-old, Christine was mated to the Bernese Osi v Allenluften who consistently produced puppies with white boots, and on March 15, 1952 she whelped four dogs and one bitch. All of the puppies were Bernese Mountain Dogs, but three of the males died soon after birth and so only Alex and Bella v Angstorf were reared. Bella had one litter later to Dani v Enggistein, and all eight puppies were Bernese. Unfortunately, Bella was euthanised at four-years-old, leaving only Alex from this litter. There was a great deal of controversy over whether Alex should be used at stud. He was an outstanding Bernese, and this was reflected in the number of show awards he accumulated. He became an International Champion and the World Champion in 1956. Gradually more people decided to incorporate Alex into their breeding plans, but each litter was carefully scrutinised. Every fault that appeared was blamed on the Newfoundland outcross, but nevertheless the overall quality of the majority of his offspring could not be denied. His owner, Herr Mischler, even considered selling the dog at one time, and he told the other breeders so at one of the meetings.

Alex sired fifty-one litters to bitches carrying a wide variety of bloodlines, and not one black puppy appeared. We can deduce that the Newfoundland colour was lost in two generations, although the influence of other Newfoundland characteristics remained with the breed. The breed improved in several ways, and for this we will be eternally grateful. Temperament improved, a deeper and broader body and chest improved the Setter-like outline seen commonly before, and the longer, straighter coat enhanced the breed in just these few generations. Line-breeding or in-breeding was still not commonly practised, but one breeder, Frau Tschanz, took advantage of the benefits that Alex could bring. Her Dursrutti Bernese have been systematically line-bred to Alex with great success, and type and consistency even after six generations of Alex's introduction to her lines is still apparent. Other breeders, especially in recent times, have followed a line-breeding or in-breeding plan – to Alex and others – with success.

CHAPTER TWO

Bernese Mountain Dogs in Switzerland Today

Today, the Schweizerischer Klub für Berner Sennenhund is one of the largest breed clubs in the country and Bernese are one of the strongest breeds numerically. The breed club organises the activities for the breed, as well as having control over which dogs and bitches are used for breeding. Dogs and bitches of fifteen-months-old and more, can attend an Ankurung, which is an assessment. These are held several times a year in each area of the country. Two assessors, who are officials of the breed club, will judge the dogs and bitches very critically for their similarity to the breed standard. Great emphasis is placed on the correct temperament, and this is tested by subjecting the dog and handler to gunfire noise and crowd situations so the assessors can see the reactions of the dog when under pressure. Hip status is also considered, only those Bernese gaining grades 0 or 1 can be considered for breeding. If the dog is considered to be a worthy specimen, then it is passed as fit for breeding for life. Those thought to be poor specimens cannot be bred from, and official pedigrees for any offspring would never be issued by the Swiss Kennel Club. The breed club would enforce a very severe punishment on anyone who bred from unregistered or unapproved Bernese, and all members of the breed club have to abide by a strict set of rules. In each area of Switzerland, the breed club has a puppy controller – Wurfkontrolle. When a litter is born, the breeder must inform the controller within three days of the birth. A Bernese bitch may rear only six puppies in a litter, and she may be bred from only once in each calendar year. So if more than six puppies are born, the excess must be culled. This has meant that there has been selection for size and markings over the years since the rules came into force, and the Swiss regard this as normal practice. Similar rules also apply to other breeds, and are enforced by breed clubs in other European countries.

The decision to rear only six puppies from a single bitch in one calendar year was made for a number of reasons. Firstly, only the very best Bernese should be kept, and since the temptation to rear every live puppy would be too great for some breeders, the breed officials agreed that some selection should take place. Secondly, six puppies, it was decided, is a suitable number for any dam to rear with little risk of her becoming over-stressed. Thirdly, Switzerland is a very small country, and with the new interest in breeding dogs which has grown this century, there could very easily be a disastrous canine population explosion if numbers were not limited. Other reasons have also been put forward, and now breeders overseas who rear more puppies in a litter are viewed with surprise by the Swiss.

In litters which contain more than six puppies, there has now been a move to involve the controller and the breeder in order to decide which puppies should be retained. At one time, litters numbering less than six would also be culled to leave only those puppies with correct markings, but now this is sometimes relaxed in certain circumstances. Of course, there are mis-marked and untypical dogs in Switzerland, and in other countries which operate such controls, but these dogs are not common. Breeders are prevented from rearing excess puppies even to be given away to pet homes with no pedigree.

The breed controllers are experienced people who can help and advise novice breeders on any aspect of the breed. Their job also involves ensuring that the premises where puppies are reared are suitable for the purpose and that hygiene standards are high. Those breeders who have proved themselves capable of rearing puppies in a good environment are awarded a commendation, but if standards fall, this can be revoked. All Bernese puppies must be tattooed on the ear-flap when they are about six-weeks-old, and this is used as a registration number, so breeders must apply to register the puppies soon after birth. The club insists that puppies must not be sold before they are eight-weeks-old, and some breeders like to keep them until they are nearer ten-weeks-old.

The system of approving judges has been carefully thought out, and only those with a long experience can be considered. Each exhibitor at a Swiss show is given a typed critique of their dog at the time of judging, and these critiques are published regularly, so the judges are open to public question if they make poor decisions or show a lack of understanding of the standard and how to judge to it. In the Bernese Mountain Dog's homeland, the breed is taken very seriously and its future has been carefully planned with the foremost aim of breeding excellent dogs. The breed club has a purpose to ensure that high standards are kept, and the club shows neither fear nor favour to anyone; the maintenance of this fine breed is the all-important objective. A desire to ensure that the working ability of the breed is kept alive has meant that training clubs and working tests are held as regularly as shows, and there is just as great a following. Veterinary experts are regularly involved in educating new owners and breeders, and the breed clubs publish regular bulletins on what is happening within the breed. It is not surprising that, even though Bernese are well established in other countries, Switzerland has retained the reputation for having the best dogs anywhere in the world. The perfect Bernese has yet to be born, but the Swiss are clear that some faults are regarded as much more serious than others. The most common faults are:

Body too small and narrow; too long. Body slabsided; too much tuck up.

Head long and narrow; head overdone with heavy loose flews, too little stop; head too domed.

Ears set too high, or held too far back; one or both ears held pricked.

Eyes too round; too light in colour; entropion.

Teeth undershot or level bite; incisors too small; missing premolars.

Neck too short.

Chest too narrow and too shallow; breastbone not pronounced.

The von Grunenmatt Litter: Astor v Chaindon – Nadja v Burgistein.
Born 22-3-1971. From this litter "Fox" came to England.

Champion Dessa v d Schwarzwasserfluh (3-4-1981)
A fine example of a mature bitch   Zbinden

Shoulders too upright.

Rump too narrow and tail set too high; curled tail.

Bone too light.

Movement poor – out at elbows; tied elbows; weak pasterns; straight stifles; 'rubber' hocks, twisted hocks, cow hocks; turned out feet.

Over white face; over white front feet; tan too pale; grey hair on featherings and grey undercoat; curly coat when adult.

Noted Breeders Of Today

Many breeders have contributed to the development of the Bernese Mountain Dog in Switzerland and it is impossible to mention everyone, but some breeders have made a mark by consistently producing excellent dogs and bitches. The Dursrutti dogs bred by Frau Tschanz have left a legacy, and her breeding successes have inspired others to follow her idea of planning ahead, rather than breeding each litter as an independent venture. Many champions bearing this affix were bred after the introduction of Alex v Angstorf into her breeding plans, and photographs of these dogs confirm that their excellent type would no doubt find favour today. Such far-thinking breeders are few and far between.

The von Sumiswald kennel of Herr Iseli was started in 1923, and continues through his son, who was President of the Swiss breed club from 1971 until 1980. Herr Iseli is still a respected judge and is regarded as one of the senior authorities on the breed. The von Grunenmatt dogs of Ernst Schlucter are bred less often these days, but are very much in demand. World Champion Asso v Hogerbuur was kennelled here and must surely rank as one of the outstanding dogs of recent years. His imposing appearance in the show ring always caused great interest, and he was a great ambassador for the breed, especially as he was a working farm dog who had to earn his keep. Xodi v Grunenmatt was exported to Eve Menegoz in Canada, and so another dynasty was formed. Fox v Grunenmatt came to England as the breed became popular, and British breeders have line-bred to Grunenmatt dogs with success.

Von Nesselacker dogs, bred by Amadeus Krauchi, are world-famous, with influential dogs acting as foundation stock throughout the world, including the USA and Great Britain. A prolific kennel, many top producers and show winners have been bred there over the past few decades, and no doubt, will continue to be bred. Josef Zumstein founded the von Oberfeld kennel in 1956, and still breeds dogs of a recognisable type. Herr Moser's Bernetta kennel also produced many champions, perhaps the most famous male being Int. Champion Hondo v Bernetta. The champion bitches Cresta and Flica both proved to be outstanding producers, but their impact on the breed was inevitably less than that of the much-used Hondo. The la Vaux dogs, bred by Herr Meister, are recognisable by a type, and both Sasso and Sandy have won consistently well and passed on their qualities to their offspring. The von Waldacker dogs, bred by Vreni Gasser, are bred from Bernetta lines, and are not only famous for their type, but also for the outstanding working ability which their breeder holds in high esteem.

CHAPTER THREE

Bernese Mountain Dogs In Great Britain

MRS Egg Leach of Switzerland first introduced the Bernese to two Samoyed breeders in Great Britain. Mrs Perry of the well-known Kobe Samoyeds based in Surrey and her friend Mrs Paterson of the Fontana Samoyeds near Edinburgh, who was the Scottish representative of the Samoyed Association, decided to establish the breed in the UK, and so our history unfolds.

The first Bernese to come to Great Britain in 1936 was the three-year-old bitch Senta v Sumiswald, bred by Herr Iseli. Owned in partnership by Mrs Perry and Mrs Paterson, she was registered by and lived with Mrs Paterson. The next Bernese to come to England were three bitches and two dogs, bought by Mrs Perry from Switzerland and released from quarantine mid-1937. Quell, a male born on November 4, 1936, Nelly, a bitch born on April 14, 1936 and the in-whelp Laura born on June 26, 1935, were all bred by Fritz Stalder of the Haslenbach kennel. Dani v d Kleinegg, born on June 5, 1935 and bred by Herr Haslebacher, and the bitch Cacilie v Ratzenberg, bred by Herr Schmid and born on November 6, 1936, completed these foundation animals. It is interesting to note that all these original Bernese were very young, and this may indicate that even then good adult Bernese with proven breeding reputations were difficult to obtain. Laura v Haslenbach had been mated to a Swiss dog Xerxes v Sumiswald bred by Herr Iseli, who was the breeder of our original Senta, and so his advice helped shape the breed in the UK from the very start. Laura whelped four dogs Alex, Bruno, Nero and Thor, and one bitch, Berna, registered of Kobe, in quarantine on March 17, 1937, and so the first litter of Bernese had been born on this island. Berna and Bruno were soon sold to Mrs Stacey, and so another pioneer of the breed would soon help establish a firm foundation for the future. In those days registered dogs could undergo a change of name when put into another home, and so Mrs Stacey re-registered both Bruno and Berna as 'of Jals'.

In 1938 Mrs Perry bred two litters from Dani v d Kleinegg and Nelly v Haslenbach increasing the Bernese population by another thirteen dogs and bitches. 1939 saw the only litter bred by Mrs Stacey, from Taurus of Kobe (from Mrs Perry's second Bernese litter) and Berna, and another two small litters from Kobe also appeared. These were the last litters bred from those early imports and their first descendants, and as war continued most of these Bernese were given away to homes where they would be well fed during such difficult times. Dani v d Kleinegg had been put to sleep after a brain tumour had been diagnosed, and Laura v Haslenbach and one or two others found places with the Army as

Miss Perry with Senta v Sumiswald, the only one of those first imports lacking white feet.

mascots. None of these dogs were bred from during the years of World War II, and so the breed died out in Great Britain after a promising start had been made to establish Bernese on these shores. But Mrs Perry's daughter retained her interest in the breed.

THE SECOND INTRODUCTION

In 1969 a male was imported from Switzerland by Mrs Jackie Sherwin. He was Hasso v Goetschiacker bred by Herr Goetschi. Mrs Sherwin, herself born in Switzerland, bought the puppy as a pet, and unfortunately for the breed he was never registered with the English Kennel Club. In fact, his existence was unknown to those about to re-establish the breed here at about the same time. Irene Creigh, a breeder of Mastiffs, came across the Bernese quite by chance, and this accidental encounter was to bring new foundation Bernese, for which we are all very grateful. Mrs Creigh exported a Mastiff puppy to Switzerland, and the delighted owner kept in touch with Mrs Creigh by sending progress reports and photographs of her pet. In the background of one of these photographs there were two Bernese, and these immediately caught the attention of the recipient. After initial investigations, Mrs Creigh and her friend Mrs Mabel Coates succeeded in buying a twelve-week-old dog puppy called Oro de Coinbarre and a twelve-month-old bitch called Dora v Breitenhof from Herr Mathez and Herr Kobel respectively, and these two were sent from Switzerland together.

During their quarantine period, a rabies alert caused all dogs to undergo a further three months enforced quarantine. Special permission was given to allow these two to be mated, and so the first litter was born in quarantine under Mrs Coates' affix Nappa. One of these bitch puppies, Black Velvet of Nappa, was to become the foundation of the Tarncred kennel owned by Mrs Lena Robbins, and Black Chiffon of Nappa was bought by Heather Curtis, who was later to import the lovely typical dog Fox v Grunenmatt from Switzerland. Oro was at this time unwell due to an adverse reaction to the rabies vaccine, and so Mrs Creigh decided to keep a male puppy for herself, in case Oro died. Fortunately, this did not happen and so the puppy Black Magic of Nappa was sold to Joyce Collis, who was later to become very famous for her Beagold Bearded Collies and in latter years her Border Collies. This dog attracted a lot of publicity as he was very successful at shows, so much so that at his first appearance at Crufts, the press photographers invaded the ring, which upset the judge, Mr Warner Hill.

The breed was given a good deal of publicity which Black Magic contributed to by appearing with Mrs Collis on the children's television programme *Magpie*. The interviewer was nearly knocked over as Berni tried to get at the cheese which the interviewer was using the attract the dog! As time went on, this dog continued to make his mark in the ring, but breeders were not keen to use him at stud, and so pressure from overseas persuaded Mrs Collis to sell the dog to Dick Schneider in the USA. When he landed at Kennedy airport, someone opened the dog's crate and Berni went missing for six weeks before he was recovered in very poor condition. Careful nursing brought him back to excellent health and condition, and when he was taken to his first show he won best of breed. Sadly, it came to an end the next summer when he succumbed to the heat and died.

Miss Perry and Major Stacey at the Birmingham National Dog Show in 1937 with the puppies Bruno and Berna of Kobe, owned by Mrs Stacey.

The first litter to be born in Great Britain in quarantine on March 17, 1937.

A mature Bruno of Jals (formerly Bruno of Kobe). Pictured in 1940.

Miss Perry at Crufts Dog Show, 1939, with Quell v Haslenbach, the Samoyed Ch. White Fang of Kobe and Nelly v Haslenbach.

Mrs Creigh imported a half-sister of Dora in 1970, Carin v Hinterfeld. It was these dogs that inspired the interest in the breed which was to grow to its present level. Carin was mated to Oro to produce the seven puppies which were the Kisumu 'A' litter, then she was sold to live out a happy life as a pet. One of her daughters, Kisumu Aphrodite had two litters for Mrs Creigh, the only other Kisumu bred litter coming from Madame Melody of Kisumu who was bred by Mrs Coates from Oro and Dora.

It was Mrs Creigh's commitment to establishing the breed which brought about the formation of the Bernese Mountain Dog Club of England, later to be changed to the Bernese Mountain Dog Club of Great Britain. Mrs Creigh started a newsletter in 1971 during her office of secretary to the club, setting a firm foundation for the breed. In 1972 Dora was given to the Guide Dogs for the Blind Association where she was bred from, and some of these puppies were sold back into the breed. One bitch puppy was successfully trained to become a Guide Dog, but it was generally felt that the breed was too slow maturing to be very successful at this work. Mrs Creigh suffered continued ill health and very soon after Oro was found a home with a friend of Mrs Creigh, and so he too enjoyed a happy retirement after having played such an important part in the breed's introduction.

Mrs Coates bred only one other litter before her interest returned fully to her first love, the English Setter. From this second litter several of the dogs and bitches found homes with people who were to become enthusiasts. Nappa Caper Caillie was sold to Hugh and Mary Horrex, who bred Bernese under the Sinova prefix, and who later imported Faro v Hurstfeld from Switzerland. Nappa Cheiron went to live with Miss Carol Lilliman, who still breeds and exhibits her Millwire Bernese. Both Nappa Confucius and Nappa Cassiopeia went to Mrs Diana Cochrane, who is still very active within the breed and whose Duntiblae kennel is famous.

Heather Curtis' Swiss import Fox v Grunenmatt was a great acquisition. Already breeding Old English Sheepdogs under the Takawalk prefix, Mrs Curtis enlisted the help of Herr Stadtman who was the patron of the Swiss Bernese Club to find a sound typical dog, and he could surely have done no better. Fox was of a type which is still greatly admired. His temperament was excellent, and this undoubtedly endeared him and the breed to others who would help the breed progress. Although not used at stud extensively, he proved to be a prepotent sire, and the Gillro dogs bred by Mrs Gillian Sharman are still recognised by the similar type they show from being line-bred to Fox's ancestors. The first challenge certificates were on offer in 1977, and Fox won two of these. He would have been sure to become a champion, but sadly his untimely death prevented this. Two of Fox's daughters out of Kisumu Aphrodite were to become the foundation bitches of the already mentioned Millwire kennel and the world-famous Forgeman Bernese still bred by Don and Brenda Griffiths.

Mr and Mrs Gray, who had been serving with the Army in Germany, came home to

Oro de Coin Barre of Kisumo and Dora v Breitenhof of Nappa with Mrs Creigh and Mrs Coates (centre), with four puppies from their first litter born 29.11.1970. Far left shows Heather Curtis with Black Chiffon of Nappa and far right is Lena Robbins with Black Velvet of Nappa.

Joyce Collis (centre) showing Black Magic of Nappa at Crufts Dog Show 1971.

Hartley Campbell

Fox v Grunenmatt. A great ambassador for the breed. Imported by Heather Curtis.

Duntiblae Nalle imported from Sweden by Mrs Diana Cochrane. Nalle appears in the pedigree of many British bred Bernese. Pictured at 10 months.   Thomas Fall

England bringing with them their dog Groll v d Leckenbecke, bred by the respected Herr Hugo Seel. Groll was used only a few times at stud, but he did pass on his qualities, producing a champion son Meiklestane Black Benjamin from a Tarncred bitch. Groll did not live to be an old dog, but he contributed to the gene pool in a valuable way. The next two imports that came to England were brought in by Mrs Diana Cochrane. An English speaking friend helped with the language difficulties and this culminated in the arrival of Nalle and Eva from Sweden. The Duntiblae prefix was added to these names, even though the dogs were bred by Eva Berndt and Mr and Mrs Stromberg respectively. Eva had four litters for Mrs Cochrane, and several of her offspring went on to win well and were subsequently used for breeding. Duntiblae Nalle caused Mrs Cochrane some concern, as he was diagnosed as suffering from osteochondritis dissecans (OCD) after lameness had occurred while he was still in quarantine. Little was known about the condition then, but Nalle made a good recovery after one of his shoulders was surgically corrected. During his show career, his soundness was commented upon and he won well, even though he was regarded as light in build. But his true worth became apparent when he was used for breeding. Nalle was the sire of the first three Champion Bernese in England – Forgeman

Folksong of Tarncred, Tarncred Puffin and Duntiblae Forgeman Fusilier. Nalle was also the sire of the first bitch to pass the BVA/KC scheme for Hip Dysplasia. No one knew at the time that Nalle would later be implicated as the dog to which all the Hypomyelinogenesis (Trembler) carriers would be traced, and so he was in-bred-on by many of the early breeders.

Imports were to appear as time went on and each gave the breed a wider gene pool, although some dogs and bitches were more influential than others. Mrs Doris Lendon, herself Swiss, brought in a bitch from Herr Pfister, Erika v Schnetzenschachen, and this bitch had four litters of Majanco's, being mated to three different Swiss imports, so again widening the genetic potential of the breed. Erika died in 1988 – the oldest Bernese in the UK at fourteen-years-old.

In 1975 John and Sonja Gorbould brought in a dog from Switzerland bred by the well known Herr Krauchi. Mustang v Nesselacker of Glanzberg was a valuable addition to the breed here. He was of excellent type, although a little short, and he consistently produced

Mustang v Nesselacker of Glanzberg, imported from Switzerland in 1975 by Mr and Mrs Gorbould. An influential sire, his son Ch. Forgeman Footpad is Gt Britain's top winning Bernese.

puppies of good type. He also caused his new owners some concern when he was struck down by heat-stroke at a show on the very day he was released from quarantine. Prompt treatment from the veterinary surgeon on duty brought about a recovery, although I am sure that his owners will never forget that episode! Although not a great winner himself, Mustang went on to sire many who did well in the ring. His most famous son was the record holding Ch. Forgeman Footpad owned by Pam Aze. His dam was Ch. Folkdance at Forgeman, the previous record holder. As the years marched on, the Gorboulds realised the value of founding some bloodlines which were unrelated to those already well established in England, and so they went on to import two more Bernese from Switzerland, and another from Norway.

Following a similar plan to establish a completely different colony of Bernese, my own imports began to arrive in 1977 with Felix v Unterzelg. A big, solid dog, he proved to be a carrier of Entropion, and so was little used at stud, as several of the blood lines already established here carried the same fault. Jumbo v Waldacker, from the well-known kennel

Champion Jumbo v Waldacker at Coliburn, the first imported Bernese, and to date the only male import to gain champion status. Owned by Brian and Jude Simonds.

of working dogs belonging to Vreni Gasser, was the next to make his mark upon the breed, gaining the distinction of being the first and only imported male to become a champion in England. His title did not come easily as he had a gay tail which was frequently penalised, and he was being shown at the time when Ch. Forgeman Footpad seemed to have the world at his feet. Rena v Lyssbach followed, and as she was of similar type and breeding to Jumbo their offspring were bound to do well. Coliburn Ember was Best of Breed at Crufts in 1983. To date, seven more imports from Switzerland have arrived at Coliburn.

THE BERNESE MOUNTAIN DOG CLUB OF GREAT BRITAIN

Since the club was started in 1971 with just twenty-five members, it has continued to grow and has been joined by other clubs for the breed. Mrs Creigh acted as secretary until 1972 when this position was filled by Mrs Diane Cochrane. The first club event was a garden party, and a grand total of twelve Bernese were present. This event was the forerunner of the very successful annual garden party which still takes place now, although aided by sponsorship. Mrs Ashfield was at this time the Patron of the Club — a fitting position as she was in fact the daughter of Mrs Perry who had imported the first Bernese into England in the 1930s. As the breed gained popularity, separate classes were scheduled at shows, and it was Mrs Ashfield who judged the first classes for the breed at Championship level.

The first club open show was held at Redditch in 1979 and the judge was Harry Glover who had shown an interest in the breed for some time. At the same time dogs were assessed by Herr Krauchi (Nesselacker) and Herr Iseli (Sumiswald) who had both been invited to attend from Switzerland. Best in Show and also announced as Best Bitch in Assessment was Carol Lilliman's Ch. Kisumu Bonne Esperance of Millwire bred by Mrs Creigh, and Best Assessed Dog was Mustang v Nesselacker of Glanzberg owned by Mr and Mrs Gorbould and bred by Herr Krauchi. In 1981 the first club championship show was held, and this event has enjoyed increased entries every year, as well as the reputation of being the most important show for the breed.

The idea of repeating the assessment held in 1979 found favour, and so two more have been held, occurring every four years. Two judges from Norway officiated in 1983, Rigmor Ulstad and Tore Fossum, and Best in Assessment was Ch. Temeraire Penny Black of Crensa owned by John and Betty James and bred by Mrs Elizabeth Wrighton. The 1987 Assessment attracted one hundred and ninety entries, and Herr Krauchi made a return visit to judge, accompanied by Herr Imhof. The Best in Assessment was Mrs Cochrane's Ch. Duntiblae Dark Protector, who carried three lines to Mrs Cochrane's first import Duntiblae Nalle. Today, the national breed club has a membership of some seven hundred, and the two open shows and one championship show held annually are supported by an increasing number of other events. Working dog days, further assessments and educational events continue to be held, and it must be hoped that the furtherance of the Bernese Mountain Dog will always be the prime objective.

The Northern Bernese Mountain Dog Club was formed in 1979 and an enthusiastic following quickly made the club a viable proposition. With the help of Sam Pascoe and established breeders such as Dorothy MacVicar Campbell, Wendy Morphet and Cynthia

Bailey, together with Maggie Davis acting as a very efficient secretary, the club made great headway. Changes on the committee have left the club with a different line-up, but a dedicated band of workers and supporters has kept the club going through some difficult times. The club gains championship status in 1991, and two very successful open shows are held every year, among other events.

In 1983 the Bernese Breeders Association of Great Britain came into being. A group of breeders and enthusiasts thought that a club for the collection and dissemination of information was needed, as little was being done in this area. This was agreed as the main objective, leaving the organisation of shows and assessments to the breed clubs. Marie Steele has been chairman since the association's formation, and I have been the secretary for the same time. Maggie Davis produces the impressive *Oasis* magazine for the group, and educational events have been organised around the country with great success. The association is the only British breed organisation to insist on compliance with a Code of Ethics as a requirement for membership. Two more clubs have also come into being in recent years: the Southern Bernese Mountain Dog Club which gains championship status in 1991, caters for the area from the south coast to the Midlands and the Scottish Bernese Mountain Dog Club.

THE LAST DECADE

The Bernese is still a relatively new breed to Great Britain and information about the breed has been hard to come by, due to language difficulties. It is impossible to mention everyone involved in this breed. But in the north of England, the most influential pioneer in those early years was Wendy Morphet, (then Fletcher) whose Meiklestane dogs were great ambassadors. Eight Meiklestane litters were born up to 1981, and even today the type is easily recognised. The prolific Inchberry kennel of Mrs MacVicar Campbell is built upon Meiklestane dogs and bitches, although the type is somewhat different. In recent years, the Meadowpark Kennel of John and Bernice Mair has consistently produced show winners for both themselves and others. Ch. Forgeman Freelance of Meadowpark, bred by Mr and Mrs Griffiths was their most important dog. He was top sire for several years and produced a very high proportion of successful show stock. Mrs Mair was also secretary of the national club for several years.

In the central area of the country, the Belynken dogs bred by Ken and Lyn Gardner have followed a set type, again easily recognised. Only twelve litters have been bred here since 1977, but the Gardners have endeavoured to follow a breeding plan and have not followed others as fashions within the breed have changed. Carol Lilliman's Millwire dogs produce only the occasional litter now, but even so they are admired for size and type by all who see them. The Gillro Bernese, bred by Gillian Sharman, are in-bred on the Grunenmatt dogs of Herr Schlucter in Switzerland, and a recognisable type consistently appears. Don and Brenda Griffiths' Forgeman Bernese are known worldwide, with many champions both at home and abroad. Ch. Folkdance at Forgeman won the Working Group at Crufts in 1980. This was truly a day to remember, as it meant that Bernese had finally made their mark among the world of pedigree dogs. Folkdance was the breed record holder, only to be eclipsed by her outstanding son Ch. Forgeman Footpad. Footpad sired only a handful of litters but he is without doubt the greatest ambassador the breed has known in the UK.

Mrs Cochrane's Duntiblae kennel began to breed Bernese in 1974, and has produced many litters right up to present times. Ch. Duntiblae Forgeman Fusilier made many friends at shows with his impressive size and steady temperament. Bred by the Griffiths, he was a son of Duntiblae Nalle. In recent years, Ch. Duntiblae Dark Protector gained the enviable achievement of being judged twice Best of Breed at Crufts. His litter sister Ch. Duntiblae Dark Pleasure has continued her winning ways since leaving the home kennel to join Mrs Haden, who now is the national club secretary. Among my own Coliburn dogs Ch. Jumbo v Waldacker at Coliburn was the first import to become a champion in the UK, and he is also the sire of champions. The ten imports have provided a combination of lines, which will hopefully prove useful to the breed in future. Most recently Tirass v Waldacker at Coliburn, who was never shown, was declared top sire in the 1987 Our Dogs/Pedigree Petfoods competition.

Julie Vaughan's Carlacot dogs have been successful in the ring for their owner, as were the Choristma dogs who came to an abrupt halt after the untimely death of their breeder Muriel Majerus. In new hands, the Choristma dogs continue to make their mark. Bred from Tarncred stock produced by Lena Robbins, this is not surprising. Lena Robbins must be regarded as one of the cleverest breeders of Bernese that this country has ever seen. Tarncreds account for the first champions in each sex in England, as well as numerous champions, both here and abroad. Litters are bred only occasionally, in common with the Forgeman dogs who come from similar ancestors, but the undoubted quality is apparent. The Glanzberg dogs of John and Sonja Gorbould have made their mark in both the show ring and as foundation stock for others. Today, the more far-seeing breeders seek not only to produce show winners, but to improve upon the soundness of this working breed. Most Bernese owners now X-ray their dogs before breeding, and the scoring scheme in operation by the BVA/KC allows breeders to know just what degree of HD is present. More and more dogs are being scored in this way, and so an increasing number of breeders are trying to use only those low-scoring dogs who carry other desired traits, when possible. Much publicity has been given to this problem, but breeders must beware not to place too much importance on this defect so allowing other problems to become established. Increased knowledge about the incidence of foreleg lameness came from a survey overseen by Dr Heather Pidduck and increased awareness of the problem will hopefully soon bring about a reduction in incidence. In 1986, Hypomyelinogenesis (Trembler) was officially recognised as being an inherited problem stemming from one bloodline within the breed. Many Bernese are in-bred on Duntiblae Nalle who appears to be the progenitor of carriers, and so the problem would appear to be widespread. No other defect has aroused such passionate views from those who have related stock and those whose Bernese are unrelated. But we can hope that as time goes on a more balanced view of the situation will bring about the best action for the continued improvement of the Bernese Mountain Dog in Great Britain.

CHAPTER FOUR

Bernese Mountain Dogs In America

THERE is evidence that the first Bernese came to Kansas in 1926. A farmer called Isaac Schiess tried to register with the American Kennel Club a dog Poincare v Sumiswald, bred by Herr Iseli (the father of the present-day Herr Iseli, still breeding under the same affix), and a bitch Donna v d Rothohe bred by Franz Schertenlieb. The AKC would not accept the registration of these dogs, and so the litter of five produced from their subsequent mating was also ineligible for registration. Even though the registrar of the Swiss Stud Book tried to convince the AKC that the Bernese were pure-bred, the AKC were adamant and so these dogs could not found a new colony.

Mrs Egg Leach, who was also instrumental in introducing the breed to England, was a sportswoman living in Switzerland. She wrote an article about the Bernese in the June issue of the *American Kennel Gazette* 1935, entitled *The Bernese is a loyal dog of the Swiss Alps*. This article caught the attention of many people, and none more than Glen Shadow of Louisiana. He wrote an article for the Western Kennel World describing how he had been enchanted by the breed as a child when he had seen pictures in a book. He had later seen the breed when he was living in France in 1918 and 1919. He got in touch with Mrs Egg Leach and the result was that on November 10, 1936 a dog and bitch arrived in America on the SS *Normandie* for Mr Shadow.

The bitch, Fridy v Haslenbach, had already proved successful as a show dog in Europe. She was awarded the CACIB, the highest award possible, at the 1935 show at Basle, and was universally accepted as a near-perfect specimen of a Bernese. The male bought at the same time, Quell v Tiergarten, was also thought to be a very nice dog, although Mr Shadow had been disappointed that the owner of a male which had particularly taken his fancy would not sell at any price, even to an American! The May 1937 issue of the *American Kennel Gazette* announced that Bernese Mountain Dogs were now recognised by the American Stud Book, and Mr Shadow's two imports were the first to be registered in the USA. In 1938 a single puppy was born to Fridy, which was duly registered as Shadows Man Friday, and in 1940 a repeat mating produced a litter of eight, four of each sex.

The choice of breed name, Bernese Mountain Dog, followed the precedent which had already been set in England. The literal translation of Berner Sennenhund – Bernese Alpine Herdsmen's dog – was thought to be too clumsy. For the next decade, Mr Shadow was the only owner and breeder of Bernese which were registered with the AKC. In all, five Bernese were imported by Mr Shadow, and he must be congratulated for his untiring efforts in establishing and popularising the breed in the USA. As in England, the War brought about difficulties, but the breed did not die out and more Bernese were registered from those original imports after 1945.

From 1941, regular attention was given to the breed with various articles and features appearing in canine journals and books and also in the *National Geographic Magazine*. The number of Bernese grew slowly but steadily, and Mr Shadow continued to extol the virtues of this breed. A wonderful story is told of the day that Mr Shadow was saved by two of his Bernese. Apparently Mr Shadow had aroused the anger of a stag, and the animal had charged, breaking four of Mr Shadow's ribs as well as inflicting lacerations and bruises. The two dogs attacked the deer from the rear, and then made a fast retreat as soon as the stag presented no further danger to their owner.

A Swiss lady living in Vermont, Miss Nelly Frey, began to breed Bernese in 1959, and by 1962 there were nine owners listed with the AKC throughout the country. Mrs Bea Knight had no luck in breeding from the first pair of Bernese she owned, but went on to import two brood bitches who helped establish her Sanctuary Woods prefix. The first realisation that Bernese were about to make big news came when the good-looking dog Ultra v Oberfeld and his owner were told by a judge at a large show: "This is a very beautiful dog, but even though I was tempted to place him I could not, as I don't know what it should look like as I have never seen one before." Bernese were at a disadvantage, because of their low entry and many judges were unsure of placing these dogs in mixed competition. However, this was soon to change when Roberta Subin's Sanctuary Woods Black Knight won fourth place in the Working Group at the Riverside Kennel Club, and so took the first three-point major win in the breed. This dog went on to become the first Champion (conformation) in the USA, although honours in the obedience ring had already been won in June 1962 when W. and M. Horstick's bitch Aya of Veralp won the Companion Dog (CD) title.

The difficulties of breeding Bernese when the breed was scattered far and wide were great, and in the early days, if travel was not a problem, then there were other reasons why matings could not go ahead as planned. Some males had low sperm counts and others died young. The heat got to some dogs and there were bitches who proved infertile or who had uterine problems. The going was not easy for these early breed enthusiasts, but by 1966 the breed had become more popular and there was a great deal of communication between those owners who were interested in ensuring a healthy future for the breed in America.

In the summer of 1967, Carol Pyle, who had been introduced to the breed by Bea Knight, set about bringing owners together to form a breed club. In January 1968 there were eight members of the club, but by the time that Mrs Pyle had sent out the club's first newsletter in March of the same year, the membership had grown to thirty-three. April 1969 saw the club's first election, and Carol Pyle was to continue as club secretary and newsletter editor. The club held a fun match in July 1970 under the organisation of Barbara Packard who was later to be influential in forming the International Bernese Register. By spring 1973 the club had gained AKC permission to hold its first sanctioned

Canadian champion Xodi v Grunenmatt, imported from Switzerland with Eve Menegoz.   Schlucter

Black Magic of Nappa, exported from the UK in 1972 by Joyce Collis.

Harriet Gehorsam with Loki and Madi v Barengraben in New Jersery.   Gehorsam

match on Cape Cod. As the breed grew in popularity, so new kennels were established throughout the States. Imports from Switzerland came into the country regularly and so the gene pool increased. The Sanctuary Woods kennel continued its breeding plans with success and many good dogs and bitches appeared bearing the Sablmate, Halidom and Mon Plaisir prefixes. The first National Speciality was held in Harrisburg, Pennsylvania in March 1976 with the wonderful entry of seventy-one Bernese. In this year the top winner for Conformation in males was the much admired Ch. Alphorns Copyright of Echo, bred by Gretchen Johnson. This male went on to be placed in the working group a total of twenty times, and was also top winning dog in 1977 and 1978. The Swiss influence was also strong as Ch. Zyta v Nesselacker bred by Herr Krauchi was top winner for conformation bitches, having won Best of Breed seven out of the eight times shown that year.

There were about three hundred and fifty members of the club by 1978, and by this time the National Speciality had become an event supported by many. The entries reached eighty-eight, which also included obedience entries, showing that the versatility of the breed was attracting interest from all sides. As the years rolled on, entries at the Speciality grew steadily, although entries at other shows were generally poor. This was due to the

Liskarn Texas Rose of Abbeycott (Butternut Right Stuff – Am. Ch Grunberg Kalais at Liskarn), born in UK quarantine kennels but conceived in America. Bred by G. Bridges and owned by D and K Wilshaw.

Bull

vast distances involved in travelling to shows, and some areas had a greater population of Bernese than others. Even today, it is not uncommon for shows, other than supported ones, to have very few Bernese entries. In the Eighties the dog to make a mark in the breed and at shows was Shersans Chang(e) O Pace owned by Robert and Carolyn Kinley and shown by their daughter Bobbi. Pace was retired in 1986, and it is some record that this dog has set for others to try to better.

As interest in the breed has grown, so has interest in eradicating or at least trying to minimise the effect of the hereditary problems within the breed. The San Francisco Bay Berners is a group of individuals who agree to breed exclusively from Bernese which are free from Hip Dysplasia, and since 1979 membership has been open to those living outside the area. Membership is only accepted from those who agree to abide by a Breeding Code (as with the Bernese Breeders Association of GB) and this interest in health matters has spread to enable the formation of the International BMD Registry founded by some members of the San Francisco Bay Berners. The Registry is indeed an exciting innovation, and there are centres in several countries now, enabling the widest circulation of information. A data-bank for recording all details about the breed, it is designed for retrospective or prospective analysis of genetic studies. Martin and Barbara Packard are the driving force behind this project, and the breed can only benefit from such a project.

AMERICAN STANDARD

General Appearance: A sturdy, balanced, large, strong-boned dog. Intelligent and having an appearance of strength and agility, suiting it to draught and droving work in mountainous regions. Dogs appear masculine, while bitches are distinctly feminine.

Head and Skull: Flat and broad with a slight furrow and a well-defined, but not exaggerated, stop.

Muzzle: Strong and straight, dry-mouthed.

Teeth: Strong, scissor bite, complete dentition. Serious fault: overshot or undershot bite.

Ears: Medium-sized, triangular in shape, gently rounded at the tip, hanging close to the head when in repose, brought forward and raised at the base when alert.

Eyes: Dark brown, slightly oval in shape with close-fitting eyelids, expression intelligent, animated and gentle. Serious faults: inverted or everted eyelids. Disqualification: Blue eye.

Neck: Strong and muscular and of medium length.

Back: Broad and firm. Topline level from withers to croup.

Chest: Deep and capacious with well-sprung ribs and brisket reaching at least to the elbows.

Body: Nearly square with overall body-length measuring slightly greater than height at withers.

Loin: Strong.

Croup: Broad and smoothly rounded to tail insertion.

Shoulders: Moderately laid back, flat-lying, well-muscled, never loose.

Forelegs: Straight and strong with the elbows well under the shoulders. Pasterns slightly sloping without weakness. Feet round and compact with well-arched toes. Dew-claws may be removed from the front legs.

Thighs: Broad, strong and muscular.

Stifles: Moderately bent, tapering smoothly into hocks.

Hocks: Well let down and straight as viewed from the rear. Dew-claws should be removed from the rear legs.

Tail: Bushy. Bone reaching to the hock joint or below. When in repose, tail should be carried low, upward swirl permissible when alert. May be carried gaily, but may never curl or be carried over the back. Fault: Kink in tail.

Coat: Thick, moderately long, slightly wavy or straight, with bright natural sheen.

Colour and markings: Tricolour – jet-black ground colour with rich rust and clear white markings. Nose always black.

Markings: (symmetry desired). Rust, over each eye, on cheeks, preferably reaching at least to the corner of the mouth; on each side of the chest; on all four legs; under tail. White, blaze and muzzle band, chest marking, typically forming an inverted cross, feet, tip of tail. Faults: markings other than described to be faulted in direct relationship to the extent of the deviation. Serious faults: white legs, white collars. Disqualification: any ground colour other than black.

Gait: Natural working gait is a slow trot, but capable of speed and agility in keeping with use in draught and droving work. Good reach in front. Powerful drive from the rear transmitted through a level back. No wasted action. Front and hind legs on each side follow through in the same plane. An increased speed, legs tend to converge toward the centre line.

Height: Dogs: 62–70 cm (24.5–27.5 in) at the withers. Bitches: 57–65 cm (22.5–25.5 in) at the withers.

Temperament: Self-confident, alert and good-natured. Never sharp or shy. A dog which will not stand for examination shall be dismissed from the ring.

Disqualifications: Blue eye-colour. Any ground colour other than black.

Scale of points:

General appearance	15
Size and height	5
Head	15
Body	15
Legs and feet	15
Tail	10
Coat	10
Colour and markings	15
Total	100

Reproduced by courtesy of the American Kennel Club.

CHAPTER FIVE

Breed Standard and Characteristics

THE physical appearance of the Bernese is striking: a dog once seen, never to be forgotten. Its stature, colouring and nobility make it a truly magnificent sight. But without the correct character and temperament, any dog which may have all the other breed attributes, is not a true Bernese. It is the character, temperament, personality and overall attitude to life which make the dog such a wonderful companion and willing worker. Attention to this aspect must be foremost in every breeder's mind if the Bernese is to retain its identity.

Bred as a general-purpose farm dog and adaptable for many tasks, the Bernese must be biddable. He should be happy to be told what to do, being most at ease when aiding and accompanying his master. He should be confident and aware of his surroundings, but he is not a loner, nor prone to take off to do as he wants. Young Bernese can be rather sensitive, and training should be undertaken by guidance, not by force. A Bernese needs to know his place from a very young age, and will never challenge his master for a dominant place in the family if his guidance has been carefully managed. Puppies which spend many hours without human company can become rather self-centred and indifferent or resentful of human attention. Sadly, a dog can develop an introvert personality from a lack of human interaction.

Bernese have a great sense of humour, a characteristic not commonly attributed to dogs; but all Bernese owners will, I am sure, endorse the fact. During training sessions, you must be careful how you react to his mistakes. Bernese love to act the clown and to be the centre of attention. If he gets a laugh when he makes a mistake, you can be quite sure that he will give repeat performances whenever an audience is present. Your Bernese will quickly assess your personality and delight in mocking you whenever he has the opportunity. My first introduction to the Bernese comic sense came from my second Bernese, a bitch called Elka. She had a stubborn streak, but overall she was very good-natured and even-tempered. I had been used to living with Border Collies, German Shepherds and working Labradors, and so was ill-prepared for her unique canine humour. During the first six months that I had her, I constantly changed my opinion as to whether she was extraordinarily stupid or was rather clever and had worked out that she could gain my sympathy by appearing not to understand me. After much observation, I realised that the latter was true, and thereafter I had no problems with her or subsequent Bernese.

Although eager to please, Bernese have a mind of their own and seem capable of reason. If there is a purpose for a particular action or training exercise, then he will happily comply. But if the action seems pointless to your Bernese, he will react stubbornly and be slow to go along with your wishes. Bernese have a true happy-go-lucky nature, they will enjoy your laughter, but they can also be sensitive and do not like to be made to look a fool or be ridiculed. Bernese are peaceable towards people, dogs and other animals, enjoying the company of all. But they will not tolerate anyone outside their own beloved family taking liberties. They are easy-going and tolerant, and many of my own adults, even the males, allow young puppies to be quite disrespectful. Young children should never be allowed to rough-handle a dog, but if this happens the Bernese rarely retaliate, preferring to move away from the offender.

They are natural watchdogs and will be quick to warn of approaching strangers or unusual happenings. But they are also capable of being very relaxed during normal day-to-day events. Bernese can be possessive and will protect their owners and their owners' belongings, but extreme provocation would be needed before a dog would rise to the occasion. It would be more inclined to bark and hold an intruder at bay, than to bite at the first opportunity. This is one of the reasons why a Bernese makes such a good family pet and companion: they are virtually one hundred per cent trustworthy in all but a panic situation.

Bernese adore people, so they are best kept as a house dog rather than confined for long periods in a kennel or run. Although active and fun-loving outside, they have a low activity level indoors, and prefer to lie in a comfortable place watching the family about their business. Inside, your Bernese will be at his happiest and most content when he is sitting next to you with a paw on your lap, or lying at your feet with his head resting on you. Bernese use their feet in a hand-like manner on their owners and others in favour. They will often put their head under your arm to get your attention if you are engrossed in a book or watching the television, and many Bernese will gently take hold of your wrist or arm in an effort to divert your attention to them. No one could ever enter a home where a Bernese lives, without the dog making its presence felt. Bernese will greet friends and family as if they have been absent for years, even if the dog sees these people frequently. Strangers are often welcomed with less enthusiasm. A Bernese should never be shy or show undue aggression, but he can sometimes be stand-offish, preferring to view strangers from his master's side. Once accepted as a friend, a Bernese will never forget you and you can always be assured of a welcome. A Bernese should never resent visitors if his owner allows them entry, but it would be a foolhardy person who tried to get past a Bernese in his owner's absence. His imposing size and deep bark make him a formidable sight. He can command respect by his very presence.

Unlike many breeds in the working group, Bernese do not require as much exercise as their size may imply. An adult Bernese will happily accompany his owner on marathon jaunts, but will not make a nuisance of himself if less exercise is the general routine. They have a real zest for life and will make the most of every opportunity, but they have the wonderful quality of being able to switch off. A Bernese will therefore be perfectly content as long as he is with the family, enjoying life and relaxing with his loved ones.

Illness can present a problem to Bernese as they often become very depressed. The dog will need to be treated like a baby and jollied along even if suffering from a minor ailment. I have known Bernese with a serious injury suffer silently, and it is well known that dogs suffering from painful shoulder or elbow conditions rarely show outward signs of pain. They just become quiet and rather introvert, so owners must be vigilant.

Physical Appearance

Although named Mountain Dog, Bernese are not comparable in size to the Pyrenean Mountain Dog or their fellow countryman, the St Bernard. One of a group of four similarly marked working dogs, the Bernese is classed as above middle-sized, according to the standard, but many people agree that they are a large breed. A Bernese should be strong and sturdy with a heavy frame, but he should also look capable of doing the general work about the farm, the purpose for which he was developed. Some Bernese do appear to be rather smaller and lighter than the standard dictates and very often these dogs have a more highly-strung temperament – not at all suitable for a farm dog. In Britain it is not uncommon to see Bernese which are more like Border Collies than typical Bernese as seen in the homeland, although variations from the ideal do appear worldwide. It can be argued that a Border Collie is a wonderful farm dog, but remember that he is bred purely as a herder, whereas a Bernese is required to do draught work, among other things.

The expression of a Bernese gives an impression of kindness and the broad head expresses strength, without coarseness. The frame is heavy for its height, and the dog should look alert but not highly strung or hyper-active. The character should be one of calmness, while retaining an alertness and interest. The colouring is spectacular, with the black, white and tan clearly defined. The black should be dense, with the top coat slightly wavy and carrying a natural sheen. The tan should be a rich chestnut colour, never pale nor brindled; and the white should be clean and bright. Freckles are sometimes seen but they should not be so obvious as to detract. Too much white makes the face appear plain, and too little can give a harsh expression. Symmetry and balance of markings are desired.

The tails of many Bernese do not conform closely to the standard. Gay tails, those carried rather higher and sometimes more curled than ideal, are very common and something that breeders are hoping to put right. Many breeders feel that a gay tail is preferable to one carried tucked under the belly; but a tail carried level with the back or hanging down in a sweep behind the dog is the most pleasing. Bernese move in a positive manner but they do not move elegantly. They should move with purpose and drive, and the limbs should move in an energy-efficient rhythm. The elbows should neither roll out, nor appear tucked in and the pasterns should flex slightly. The hind-legs should be well angulated without being over done and the hocks should be firm and strong, with little or no sideways movement. The hindquarters should follow through with drive, and viewed from the front and rear the legs should be parallel, converging nearer the centre line the faster the dog moves. Free, effortless movement is essential in a working dog, as without this he would be useless to the farmers who employ him.

BRITISH BREED STANDARD

General Appearance: Strong, sturdy working dog, active, alert, well boned, of striking colour.

Characteristics: A multi-purpose farm dog capable of draught work. A kind and devoted family dog. Slow to mature.

Temperament: Self-confident, good-natured, friendly and fearless. Aggressiveness not to be tolerated.

Head and Skull: Strong with flat skull, very slight furrow, well-defined stop, strong, straight muzzle. Lips slightly developed.

Eyes: Dark brown, almond-shaped, well-fitting eyelids.

Ears: Medium sized, set high, triangular shaped, lying flat in repose, when alert brought slightly forward and raised at base.

Mouth: Jaws strong with a perfect, rectangular and complete scissor bite, i.e. upper teeth closely overlapping lower teeth and set square to the jaws.

Neck: Strong, muscular and medium length.

Forequarters: Shoulders long, strong and sloping, with upper arm forming a distinct angle, flat-lying, well muscled. Forelegs straight from all sides. Pasterns flexing slightly.

Body: Compact rather than long. Height to length 9:10. Broad chest, good depth of brisket reaching at least to elbow. Well ribbed, strong loins. Firm, straight back. Rump smoothly rounded.

Hindquarters: Broad, strong and well muscled. Stifles well bent. Hock strong, well let down and turning neither in nor out. Dew-claws to be removed.

Feet: Short, round and compact.

Tail: Bushy, reaching just below the hock. Raised when alert or moving but never curled or carried over back.

Gait/Movement: Stride reaching out well in front, following well through behind, balanced stride in all gaits.

Coat: Soft, silky with bright natural sheen, long, slightly wavy but should not curl when mature.

Colour: Jet black, with rich reddish-brown on cheeks, over eyes, on all four legs and on chest. Slight to medium-sized symmetrical white head marking (blaze) and white chest marking (cross) are essential. Preferred but not essential, white paws, white not reaching higher than pastern, white tip to tail. A few white hairs at nape of neck and white anal patch undesirable but tolerated.

Size: Dogs: 64–70 cm (25–27½ in) Bitches: 58–66 cm (23–26 in).

Faults: Any departure from the foregoing points should be considered a fault and the seriousness with which the fault should be regarded should be in exact proportion to its degree.

Note: Male animals should have two apparently normal testicles fully descended into the scrotum.

Under-marked.

Over-marked.

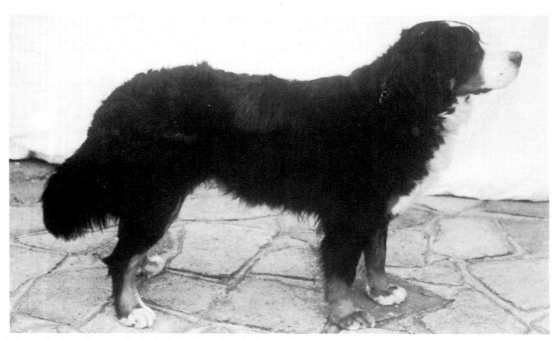

Untypical male, too light in build and unbalanced.

Bitch showing untypical head –
Appenzeller-like.

Narrow front.

Poor hind angulation and stance.

Champion Forgeman Footpad at five-months-old.   Aze

. . . and as an adult. Top UK winner, owned by Pam Aze.   Aze

CHAPTER SIX

Your First Bernese

OWNER SUITABILITY

IF you have decided that a Bernese should join your family, then you will be eager to find a puppy or older dog as soon as possible. But dog ownership is a very real commitment of time, expense and above all, responsibility. I think that spending time with your Bernese is the most important factor in establishing a happy relationship, yet time is the commodity that most owners lack. Bernese are devoted to people and rely on daily affection and attention from their owners. Even the company of another pet is no substitute for the human Bernese relationship. If it is likely that your daily schedule will prevent you spending time with your Bernese, then consider postponing your purchase until the situation changes.

All dog lovers will tell you that Bernese make wonderful companions. But there are times when things are not so good. An owner's responsibilities include dealing with illness, death and possibly euthanasia, so a commonsense attitude is a must. Sentimentality is a part of most people's characters but strength is also needed. Bernese are not noted for longevity: seven or eight years is the average life expectancy. Although this is not a very long time in life terms, these years can be a burden if you are not prepared to shoulder the full responsibilities of dog ownership.

Thought must be given to other basic requirements: food, accommodation, training and health care must also be planned. The cost of feeding a Bernese can vary according to the type of food provided. Puppies need good-quality food for health and growth, and economies cannot be made. Growing youngsters eat more than adults but, even so, the weekly food bill for an adult Bernese is a factor to consider in family finances. Veterinary care is another expense to budget for. Preventative medicine such as vaccinations, flea and worm control will be a regular occurrence and your dog is likely to need some treatment for ill health during its life. Insurance can be sought to cover some of the expense but obviously a premium must be paid. Third party insurance cover is also necessary in case your Bernese should cause an accident or damage property.

YOUR FAMILY LIFESTYLE

It is wise to consider your family's commitments and the impact that the addition of a new puppy will have on the established routine. Special allowances can be made for a puppy but to enjoy your Bernese to the full, you should plan well ahead. If your adult Bernese does not fit easily into your lifestyle, then trouble is bound to occur. Every member of your family must agree and genuinely want a dog to join the home. It is possible to involve your dog in most activities, but how will you arrange care for your Bernese when you are out? Bernese love to travel with the family so a car which is suitable to carry the dog and the family seems obvious but is often overlooked.

Bernese do not like to be alone for long periods on a regular basis, so someone should be at home for the best part of each day. If everyone in the family works full-time, a Bernese would be an unwise acquisition. After a hard day at work, the last thing anyone wants is a Bernese demanding attention. Apart from feeding and clearing up after the puppy, there must be a firm commitment to training. If the person taking overall responsibility also has young children to care for, then the addition of a puppy could prove too demanding. If you enjoy an orderly house, then the disruption caused by a puppy is a drawback. There is no need for any dog to have access to all the rooms in the house, but be prepared for a trail of dust, dirt and hair where the dog is allowed to go. Puppies also take time to toilet train and so accidents are bound to occur. You can never be quite so house proud once a dog has joined the family. A landscaped garden may also suffer from the attentions of a Bernese puppy or adult, so you must either take a more flexible attitude or fence off an area where the dog can do no damage.

WHEN TO BUY

Plan well in advance the right moment to acquire your Bernese. Most people find it easier to rear a puppy during the spring and summer months but your own commitments and plans should influence when you take a Bernese into your home. Wanting a dog is not a good enough reason for getting a dog. It is not fair on you, the dog or neighbours to leave it unattended while everyone is at work during the day. No amount of attention in the evenings will compensate for the boredom experienced by the dog during enforced solitary confinement. It is much better to wait until someone can work part-time or give up work completely.

If a house move is planned, it may seem reasonable to get a puppy when the new house is in a mess. This could work but it is likely that you will not have much time to spend with the dog if work is needed on the new house. It is better to wait until you are settled before introducing a new pet. If you are planning building work or maybe some structural alterations to your home, be sure to get the work completed. Apart from the obvious hazards to a dog, a routine cannot be established with workmen on the premises and a puppy may find the upheaval too much to cope with. Some people like to rear a child and a puppy together. This can be very beneficial to both but it is also a great demand upon the mother of the family. If a new baby is planned, wait until the child is of an age when it will be easier to cope with the demands of a puppy. Too many dogs are rejected when a child is born into the family. It is better to wait until after the baby is born to see if you can cope with the extra responsibility of a puppy.

Finally, if you are taking a young puppy into your home during the summer months, arrangements must be made if you are going away on holiday. Young puppies should not be boarded in kennels and even those under twelve months are not happy in these establishments. The noise and routine can leave a youngster feeling very confused and the lack of individual attention during formative months may disrupt your training plans. Adults accept kennel situations more easily. But young Bernese often acquire the habit of barking if left at noisy premises for any length of time. A trusted friend or relative may be able to look after your pet while you are away, but by far the best solution is to organise someone to come and stay at your house to look after your Bernese. This will allow your puppy to continue his routine and habits with the least disruption, which must augur well for your return to training.

FACILITIES

Most owners want their Bernese to live as part of the family and, given the choice, that is what your Bernese would opt for. Human companionship is a Bernese's first priority and this is most freely available when the dog is living alongside you. Although a large breed, Bernese do not need a great deal of room so a large house is not necessary for its comfort. However, a place of its own to retire to after walks and games is important. This could be a corner of the kitchen or a utility room or a similar spot, just a little away from the main traffic of the family. Bernese do not feel the need to rush about indoors. They prefer to keep a low activity level inside and are more active when outside.

Access to a garden or yard is essential. Exercise can obviously be arranged off the premises and this gives another opportunity to spend time with your pet on a one-to-one basis. But between walks there must be somewhere for your Bernese to relieve itself, and also a place to play or just lie out to get some fresh air. Young Bernese will make use of a large garden for play and exploration but most adults prefer to lie near the house to enable them to see and hear what is happening inside. Facilities to dispose of excreta must also be given some thought. Perhaps a site to install a sunken dog loo can be investigated or disposal via the sewage system may be an option. Although Bernese are not particularly athletic, they are well able to clear a fence, so it is necessary to have a suitable barrier to keep your dog on your own premises. Do not expect your puppy to respect other people's property!

FINDING A BREEDER

Names and addresses of breeders are available from a number of sources. Puppy agencies keep a list of breeders but these are compiled on a fee-paying basis and not by maintaining any particular standard. Breed clubs also keep lists of members and these are also readily available but again, there is no indication of the quality of Bernese or the reputation of the breeders. In Great Britain, only one breed association applies a code of ethics as a requirement of membership. Advertisements in weekly canine publications or breed magazines may offer some ideas as to the show record of dogs and puppies for sale. But even though you may be aware of the breed standard, you will not be able to appreciate the differences between family strains of the breed until you have seen a number of Bernese from a variety of breeders.

The ideal opportunity to compare different types is to visit a show where Bernese are scheduled. Details of shows can be obtained from the canine weekly papers, or breed clubs. One trip to a show could give you the chance to see dogs from all over the country so is well worth the effort in your quest for the ideal Bernese. Even if you are not interested in showing or breeding yourself, you will soon appreciate that some types or families of Bernese appeal to you much more than others. These differences are not so easy to spot in puppies, so it is best to have a good look, as much can be learned from studying adults.

VISITING A BREEDER
Most breeders of Bernese keep their dogs as a hobby, although some breed for profit. In both cases, they will be looking after dogs as well as running a household. So your visit will be timed to cause the minimum disruption to routine. Punctuality on your part will be much appreciated. I cannot begin to remember how many hours I have wasted waiting for people to arrive to visit the dogs. It can sometimes be difficult to time your arrival exactly, especially if travelling some distance. But if you are delayed, a telephone call will be gratefully received. A little consideration will certainly endear you to the breeder.

All the family may be keen to view the dogs, but I do feel that it may be far more sensible to leave the children with a minder while you visit the breeder's premises. It will be far easier for you to absorb the information you are given without the distraction of the children. Children, especially young children, become bored within a very short time and may well become disgruntled or start to wander. If dogs on the premises are not used to children, this could be a problem. Although Bernese are usually very gentle with children, children are not always very gentle with other people's Bernese. Dogs not used to the noise and excitement generated by small children may not react favourably.

When you arrive, ask to see the adult dogs before you look at the puppies. It is one thing to see a number of dogs at a show to get an idea about a breed, but spending some time with one or more large dogs within a household can be an enlightening experience. Bernese always seem larger when seen in a room at armchair level and so by looking at adults in this way first you can be more objective. The adult Bernese should approach you without fear or aggression and be keen to investigate you. Most Bernese will, in fact, greet you as a long lost friend, but a slightly less enthusiastic greeting does not indicate a faulty temperament. The temperament of the adults you meet will give you an indication of the temperament likely to be inherited by puppies bred from similar bloodlines. It will also show you how the breeder handles and socialises her dogs. It will be clear if the dogs are loved as pets or kept merely as viable financial stock. If a breeder gives a lot of attention to her adults, she is likely to spend a lot of time handling puppies and so accustoming them to people before they leave for their new homes.

The temperament of puppies which have been reared in the house may differ from those which have been kept in kennels. I believe that kennel-reared puppies are often at a disadvantage when they go to their new homes. They have to get used to unfamiliar surroundings, the continual presence of people and all the strange household noises and smells. If kennel-reared puppies have been allowed to spend some time in a house before leaving for a new home, then they will adapt more easily. A puppy's attitude towards people can also be affected by kennel rearing. Behaviour patterns which are evident at seven or eight weeks of age are not necessarily adopted throughout adult life, but human interaction between three and six weeks of age is known to have great influence on future personality.

Kennelled dogs and puppies usually spend a lot of time without human company and this can set off a number of reactions. A dog that gets wildly over-excited when allowed to be in company of people may prove difficult to manage. A timid-fearful approach can be due to too little human contact and will mean that a puppy will take much longer to settle into new surroundings. Some puppies, with a good inherited temperamental background, may become rather indifferent to people. These puppies usually prove very difficult to train as they are somewhat self-centred and fail to accept human dominance. Most owners want a pet that is interesting but easy to live with. A sensible attitude to people and the ability to settle down, are the qualities most desired in the breed.

DOG OR BITCH?

The sex of the puppy you will buy may be of little consequence to you but careful thought should be given to this aspect. If you already have a dog in residence, then you would be wise not to mix the sexes of entire animals. Separation during a bitch's seasons will cause great disruption to a normal family routine and is not fair on either dog. Many people do cope admirably, but you have to provide facilities not only to prevent an unwanted mating but also to avoid frustration. If you want to keep both sexes and have no plans to breed, the bitch should be spayed. Castration of the male will not solve the problem of sexual awareness when a bitch is in season, so is a less viable option.

In some breeds, there is a great difference between the sexes. Males are often more dominant than bitches and rather assertive. Generally speaking, this is not the case in Bernese, although some bloodlines do produce individuals which can be more active and highly-strung – but this affects both sexes. Many of the established breeders, myself included, prefer the temperament of males to bitches as they are not prone to hormonal changes affecting character. The main differences are:

MALES	BITCHES
Larger and more impressive.	Smaller and lighter built.
Moult once yearly.	Moult twice yearly.
Urine-mark territory.	Urine scorches lawn.
Can be sexually aware.	Seasons twice-yearly.
More expensive to feed.	More competition at shows.
Faster growth-rate increases risk of bone problems.	Risk of hormone imbalance causing problems of womb, false pregnancy etc.

Spaying or castration can alter the moulting cycle; sexual awareness, hormone imbalance and territory marking can also be lessened by such operations. So we come down to size as being a major factor when choosing the sex. I am a believer in neutering pet dogs and bitches as it makes them easier to manage in novice hands. In an ideal world these

Adult dog and bitch showing difference in size.

Habits learned as a puppy will continue in adult life.   Brown

measures would not be necessary. But in reality, pet dogs, which means the large majority of the dog population, are easier to manage and so can lead happier lives as part of a family. There are so many unwanted puppies produced throughout the world, through ignorance or misguided sentimentality, that I feel early neutering could at least slow down the population explosion. Breeding is a long-term commitment to a breed, and to *all* puppies produced. This should not be taken on lightly.

ONE DOG OR TWO?

Bernese, in common with some other breeds, like the company of other dogs although not as a substitute for human attention.

Owners can derive a great deal of pleasure from seeing two dogs playing together and watching their relationship develop. Because Bernese, especially puppies, are so charming, many owners decide at some time to keep two together. But it is not advisable to buy two puppies at the same time. It may, in theory, seem a good idea to have two that can be playmates for each other. I have done this on several occasions with success. But you rarely get such a good human/dog relationship when you are rearing two youngsters, as you do not have a one-to-one relationship. All puppies need a lot of guidance to instil behaviour patterns for the future and it is essential to be able to hold the puppy's attention. Two puppies reared together are always more interested in each other than their owner. House training, lead training and general behaviour in the house are easier when dealing with one puppy at a time. It is far more rewarding to get the formative training well established with one puppy, so that he can act as an example to another. I think that a minimum of nine months age difference is about right for most inexperienced owners to aim for and this has worked well for several owners that I know.

Bitches are naturally maternal and usually accept the arrival of a puppy eagerly. The difference in size must be considered and so energetic games between a young puppy and an older, much heavier and clumsier dog must be carefully supervised. Two males can also live happily together and perhaps in these situations an age difference helps to establish a pecking order. Lifelong compatibility can be assured if the newcomer learns from the start that he is the underdog and this is naturally accomplished by a sensible age difference. Bernese are a heavy, slow-maturing breed. There is always some risk of growth problems with any Bernese puppy, but these risks are increased when more than one dog lives on the premises. Some problems are wholly inherited, but management plays a large part in the occurrence of some conditions. Puppies can injure each other and can easily be injured by older dogs. Increased activity stimulated by the presence of another dog can lead to growth problems in some puppies, and so careful management and a sensible owner-attitude is a must for homes with more than one dog.

Sometimes, owners of an old dog feel that they would like to introduce a new puppy into the house before the old dog dies. When you are used to living with a dog, it is a very uncomfortable feeling to be left alone when a loved companion dies. Whether it is right to bring a new puppy into the company of a very old dog is something that each individual must decide. Often, the arrival of a newcomer can perk up an old dog and give a new lease of life, as long as the puppy is not allowed to become a nuisance to the old dog. But if the established pet has lived as the only dog in the family for all of its life, introducing a puppy may be regarded as cruel. How would you feel if, in your twilight years, you were suddenly confronted with your replacement?

BOOKING A PUPPY

After visiting a breeder, you may have decided that a Bernese really is the breed for you. Whether that particular breeder has the type of dog which appeals to you, is a matter of choice, but at least you are sufficiently aware of the breed to make a considered decision. Once a suitable breeder has been located, then a firm booking can be made. It may be possible to choose a puppy which is ready to leave for its new home straightaway. To avoid disappointment, it is wise to make sure that the breeder knows your requirements and that you are aware of your position on the waiting list if there is one.

Some breeders are more keen to sell their puppies into homes where they will be shown or bred from, so effectively advertising the breeder's stock. Often, these breeders have puppies which are less than perfect in some way and these are offered to pet customers. The defect can be as minor as slightly less than perfect markings and many people are happy to give a home to these puppies. But, personally, I see no reason why pet customers should be offered only the lesser quality puppies. I would much rather sell the puppies, considering new owner suitability of course, on a first come first served basis. Consideration can be given to prospective owners who have an interest in future showing or breeding but I should like to reverse the attitude that a pet puppy is a sub-standard puppy. Breeders should be happy to find permanent, caring homes for their puppies, regardless of whether they are of a show potential or not. Some prospective purchasers may be more interested in puppies sold more cheaply due to imperfections, but equal opportunity should be offered to all, when puppies are priced the same.

Interested purchasers should beware of the new trend in selling puppies on breeding terms or stud terms arrangements. Joint ownerships are also commonly offered to new owners but be cautious before entering into any kind of contract which may affect your rights and future decisions. Breeding terms is in effect, a lease or hiring agreement which enables the breeder to use your bitch for breeding. I have heard breeders tell prospective owners that the only way of obtaining a good quality Bernese bitch is by entering into such an agreement as no breeder can afford to part with a good bitch outright. This is nonsense and should be dismissed. Breeding terms agreements vary from breeder to breeder and some are overseen by the Kennel Club or legal personnel. Basically, you will be asked to sign an agreement allowing your bitch to be used for breeding, with a sire of the breeder's choice. The breeder will then be entitled to one or more puppies. Individual arrangements are made as to whether the bitch stays with you, giving you the expense of rearing the puppies, or whether she is kept by the breeder while the litter is whelped and the puppies are reared. Either way, breeding terms are not always in the best interest of the bitch or purchaser. Until the contract is fulfilled, the dog is not wholly yours.

Stud terms are also becoming fashionable but this can leave an owner with unforeseen problems. Male Bernese, which are wanted as a family companion, are best kept ignorant of sexual activity. Bernese males are not especially interested in bitches, although we have all seen some dogs which seem to think of nothing else! But to allow a male to mate a bitch, whether it be often or infrequently, is a decision which cannot be taken lightly. Stud terms allow the breeder to arrange for bitches of his choice to be mated to your male whenever the need arises. Some males undergo little or no change of attitude after mating a bitch. They may remain as loving and responsive as they were before the event. I have kept as many as six males, all used for breeding, at the same time and they lived quite happily in the company of bitches without being a nuisance to each other or showing more sexual awareness on outings outside the home. But many owners have used a dog for breeding just once, and then seen unfortunate character changes in their dog. If the decision to breed from your male has been considered carefully, after assessing his adult potential and character, then you have only yourself to blame if your are left with a somewhat frustrated sex maniac. If the decision has been made by a third party, the breeder, then it is still you and your family that have to cope with changes of attitude left as a legacy from the agreement.

Joint ownership, or partnerships, are sometimes offered to prospective purchasers who may want to buy a Bernese to campaign in the show ring. If a breeder has a promising youngster but has little or no time to show the dog herself, then she may offer the youngster to a keen newcomer. These arrangements are becoming increasingly common, as any show catalogue will confirm, and indeed in the USA many dogs are owned jointly. Individual contracts should be carefully screened before making a decision. Personally, I do not agree with contracts which may affect the ownership of a dog if a disagreement occurs. If a breeder wants to retain an interest in an individual dog or bitch badly enough, then it seems appropriate to keep the dog on the home premises. If a keen newcomer wants to breed or show a dog, then I am sure that there are plenty of breeders who will sell a promising puppy outright. We wouldn't dream of adding a new member to our own family by lease, so why should we do it to gain a Bernese?

CHOOSING A PUPPY

Some breeders prefer to postpone the final choice until it is time for the puppy to be collected to go to its new home. Many breeders advise that five or six weeks old is the ideal time to choose from a litter. Before this age, choice can only be made from markings and size, both of which will change as the puppy grows. Although the physical appearance of your puppy should be pleasing, it is the temperament and character of your pet which will have a day-to-day effect on your home life and so temperament must be your first consideration. Individual character is difficult, if not impossible to assess before four weeks old, so by six weeks the personality will be more apparent.

CONSIDERING BREED POINTS

When a Bernese puppy is to be a family pet, owners may place little importance on breed points as set out in the breed standard. Most people know immediately whether a puppy

Look carefully at all the puppies before making a final choice.   Hodge

Puppies need to investigate everything!   Spink

appeals to them or not. However, if you are hoping to show or eventually breed from your Bernese, then more care should be taken to study each puppy, maybe even comparing it against the breed standard. Obviously, most people would like to own the best puppy in a litter but this is not possible for everyone. If you are looking for a potential breeding Bernese, then the overall quality of the litter is of prime importance. A litter of puppies which are similar in size, shape, type and markings is more likely to contain Bernese which will go on to breed true to type, than an individual which stands out among varied and undistinguished littermates. A one-off rarely goes on to produce a high proportion of quality Bernese. No matter what the puppy is destined to be, a sound temperament must be your first consideration. Even the most beautiful dog is impossible to live with if it has a faulty character. Health and correct construction is the second factor to influence your choice and breed points, if all correct, are the icing on the cake.

The striking tan and white markings on a basically black dog are a feature which attract many owners to the breed. Sometimes puppies are born with less than perfect markings, but these puppies are the same as the more classically marked puppies in every other way. Markings can deviate from the standard in a number of ways: too much or too little white on the face and legs, white hairs in varying proportions on the back of the neck or around the anus, or facial markings which are not symmetrical. Deviations of this nature should be taken into account, but do not overlook a puppy which is superior to the others in every other way, except in its markings.

Once the overall impression of the litter has been noted, the breeder should remove the puppies which have been booked already and those of the sex you do not want, to make it easier to study those you can choose from. Bernese puppies can be rather lazy so watch each puppy as it moves around. Apart from the general health points mentioned, take time to note the individual characteristics of each puppy. Try not to be too hasty to reject a puppy from further consideration for what may be a minor reason. The size of any individual does not necessarily indicate the stature upon maturity. The biggest puppy rarely grows into the largest adult and the smallest may grow to the same size as its littermates. The proportions of a Bernese puppy are a more reliable indicator of potential size. The thickness of the bones, always heavier on the front legs, and the lengths between joints – front foot to pastern, hind foot to hock – will help you to decide, if maximum size is an important factor. A puppy which appears broader than its littermates will probably keep a solid sturdy outline as an adult, but be sure it really is broader across the chest and body and not merely carrying a full stomach!

THE IDEAL BERNESE PUPPY
A typical Bernese puppy should look rather square and solid at first glance. Adults are slightly longer than they are high but puppies should look square because of the rather profuse coat. At six-weeks-old, the pup should stand with its feet set squarely on the ground and its head carried well up on a strong neck. Although they should move freely, Bernese puppies are not exactly elegant and you are likely to witness several puppies in any litter tripping over themselves in their enthusiasm to beat their littermates to reach an

attraction. There should be good width between the limbs, and viewed from the front, the front legs should look straight from top to toe, neither turning in nor out. Puppies sometimes tend to turn their feet out slightly, but this usually improves as the puppy grows and gains more co-ordination and muscle control. Unlike some large breeds, Bernese puppies do not usually exhibit large joints from which you can predict size. The hindlegs are never quite so heavily boned as the front, but the hocks (ankles) should look strong and hind dew-claws should be removed. Viewed from the rear, there should be a similar distance between the hocks and between the feet. If the hocks converge, then it is likely that the dog will be cow-hocked as an adult to a greater or lesser degree. The feet should point forward. Hind feet which turn out is a common fault within the breed, but it doesn't affect the way the dog functions. Some adult Bernese seem to have hocks which are twisted outwards, so giving the appearance that the toes are set on the outside edge of the foot. Again, to my knowledge this rarely affects the dog to any extent, but should be viewed as more serious if you are hoping to breed later on. Certainly, the fault is transmitted through generations.

A Bernese puppy's head should seem rather large compared to body size. It should be broad, both across the top of the head and through the cheeks and muzzle. The fluffy puppy coat can often conceal the real shape, so cup your hands either side of the head to see the true outline. The ears also appear rather large and I always think that this is a good sign as it often means that the puppy will reach a good adult size. The stop, the drop from the top of the head to the muzzle, should be steep and pronounced. During teething periods, the stop will often decrease and then return later on in the final growth stages. But in a six-week-old puppy, a deep stop is desired. A puppy lacking in stop appears to have a wedge-shaped head when viewed in profile and will rarely improve in this point. The muzzle should ideally be short and blunt, looking like a cube on the front of the head. Long muzzles and narrow, snipy jaws never improve in my experience. The white markings on the head can be rather misleading when trying to determine head shape, so bear this in mind. Novice Bernese enthusiasts are perhaps best advised to look for a teddy bear or panda-shaped head, as opposed to one that looks fox-like.

The eyes should be almond-shaped, although in young puppies they do appear a bit rounder, but they should be very dark. Newly opened eyes are navy blue and change to brown at around eight to ten-weeks-old, sometimes later. Some Bernese have wall eyes, a lack of pigment which makes one or both eyes white. This does not affect vision at all but it does give a rather cold expression. A puppy which has a wall eye will have brighter blue coloured eyes than the others which may still be at the navy blue stage. Close inspection will reveal a white ring around the pupil of the eye and this is the iris which is lacking in pigmentation. A puppy with one or two wall eyes should be sold for less than the perfect puppies in the litter. Interestingly, wall eyes are most commonly seen in puppies which have excessive white markings on the head. In some countries a wall eye would exclude a Bernese from show ring competition but in England I have seen one bitch shown in breed classes with this fault. A Bernese with this fault will not always produce the same fault in future generations but is best avoided if you have ambitions to breed Bernese.

A watery or thick discharge from the eye may indicate infection or possibly entropion, which is more serious and very painful for the dog. Entropion is a turning in of the eyelids, which causes irritation and ultimately ulceration of the eyeball. This is a hereditary defect and although it can be surgically eased by one or more operations as the dog develops, any puppy showing this deformity should be rejected by the prospective purchaser. Occasionally, a puppy may be seen with pronounced third eyelids. These are flaps of skin formed at the inner edge of the eye and are a natural part of the dog. If an eye is inflamed or sore, the third eyelid comes across over the eye to act as a natural protection. If the membrane is obvious, it may indicate some irritation which warrants further scrutiny. This third eyelid is often dark in colour, blending in with the colour of the eye. But it can also be lacking in pigment and appear pale and opaque. Again, this does not affect the function of the eye, but it does look rather ugly.

The puppy's nose may be cold and wet but often puppies have rather warmer, dryer noses than some manuals state. As long as there are no signs of discharge and the puppy is happy and active, there is no cause for concern. The pigmentation of the nose may be complete, so showing completely black, but quite often puppies don't complete pigmentation around the nose for some time. I have never known a nose to remain pink and unpigmented on a Bernese but that doesn't mean that it doesn't happen. Bernese with excessive white markings are more likely to have slower developing pigmentation than those with classic markings, and undermarked puppies, those with less than ideal white markings, rarely, if ever, have poor pigmentation. Generally speaking, a classically marked puppy of about six-weeks-old should have at least half of the nose coloured black if it is to be correctly pigmented as an adult. Less than that could well develop correctly in time, but there is more risk. The pigment usually advances from the centre of the nose outwards.

The pigment of the mouth and inner lips and gums is usually a mixture of pink and black patches, so there is no need to worry unduly here. But close inspection of a puppy's mouth is necessary before purchase. At six weeks, I would expect the teeth to be well through the gums and evenly spaced. Crowding of the teeth in an adult Bernese is commonly seen and can be noticed sometimes in puppies. Many Bernese do have rather small incisors, the centre front teeth on the bottom jaw, and it is these teeth which are the most likely to be displaced. If the incisors are placed ahead or behind the teeth either side, it doesn't mean the dog will have an incorrect bite later on but the risk of deviation is increased.

The canine teeth, sometimes called the eye teeth, should fit well together with the top canines fitting snugly behind the lower canines. The incisors of the top jaw should fit neatly over the lower incisors with little or no visible gap. A slightly imperfect bite will cause no problems to a companion Bernese, but should be avoided if you have other plans. Dentition faults most commonly seen in Bernese are: an overshot bite, when the teeth on the top jaw, or indeed the jaw itself, protrudes over the bottom teeth by up to a quarter or even half of an inch; an undershot bite, when the lower teeth or jaw extend too far forward ahead of the upper teeth; and a level bite, when the incisor teeth meet edge to edge. These faults are seen in puppies but more usually develop during the five to ten-month-old period. The most serious dental defect that a puppy can show is an overshot bite with the canine teeth in a reverse position – the upper canine in front of the lower canine. This situation rarely improves and the lower canines often push into the roof of the mouth causing discomfort to the puppy. A Bernese puppy with this fault should not be chosen as its future is bound to be complicated.

Puppies often carry their tails higher than is seen on an adult. They use it as a rudder to help balance and as a useful handle to catch hold of littermates! The tail should be set on low so that the outline of the back flows into the tail smoothly. A tail which is set too high so that it protrudes out of the rump in an upward direction will doom the dog to carry the tail high throughout its life. The tail should reach at least to the tip of the hock joint and ideally just below that joint. Some puppies may have a kink to the tail and this will be penalised as a show fault.

The puppy's coat should be profuse and thick. It will not be shiny in a young puppy but it should be clean. A smoother coat is sometimes seen and as long as it is dense and has a good undercoat, this is not necessarily a point to cause concern. I prefer a puppy with a shaggy coat but buyers should remember that puppies which have had good access to plenty of fresh air often show heavier coats than those reared almost entirely indoors. Many breeders have experienced incidence of dandruff or scurf on puppies. This can be caused by a mite infestation but such a dense coat can also invite such a symptom. It usually clears up completely as the coat changes.

The tan marking on puppies is much paler than it is on adults. As the puppy matures, the colour will darken to a rich reddish tan. Black markings at the base of the toes are sometimes seen on puppies with little or no white on the feet. The tan colour under the root of the tail is often even a shade or two paler than seen on the legs. A grey shading has been seen on Bernese puppies and adults and although a serious breed fault, it is of minor importance for a companion puppy. The shading appears on the trousers at the rear of the hind legs and is sometimes noticed on the tan of the legs and running through the black hair on the back. It can disappear with maturity but should be considered a fault for a potential show or breeding dog.

The extent of white markings on a Bernese puppy comes down to personal preference. The breed standard clearly states that head markings should be slight to medium-sized but even so, this is open to interpretation. Most owners prefer a puppy with a lot of white on the face as this is most eye-catching. All things being equal, I am sure most people prefer to have a Bernese with classic markings. The set pattern of the tri-colour markings is an important feature of the breed but I feel that too much emphasis has been, and is, placed on this aspect. A Bernese without tan or white markings would not be a true Bernese but an overall solid, typical dog should not be overlooked because of minor marking deviations.

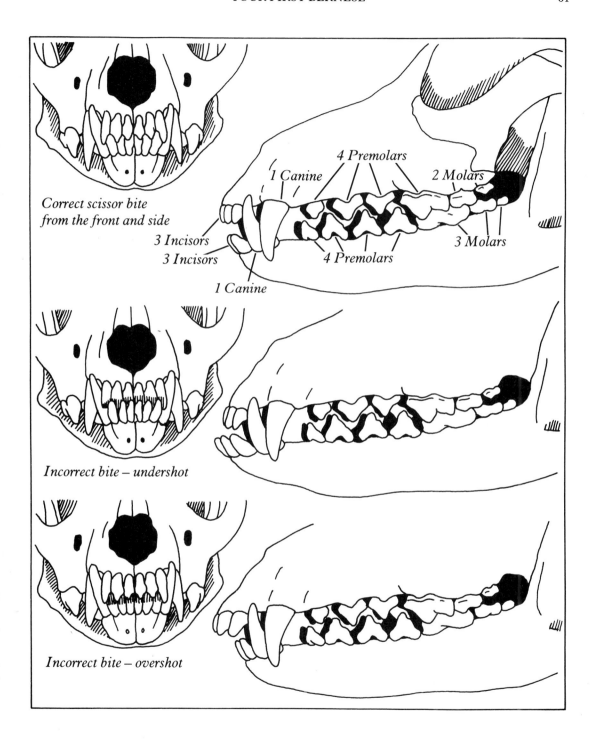

Correct scissor bite from the front and side

1 Canine

4 Premolars

2 Molars

3 Incisors

3 Incisors

4 Premolars

3 Molars

1 Canine

Incorrect bite – undershot

Incorrect bite – overshot

CHAPTER SEVEN

Initial Training

Bernese like to be the centre of attention, and from a training point of view, they are usually attentive. Puppies can be easily distracted, so training sessions must be short to be effective. Many owners fail to realise that every time they talk to their pet, and every time they do something with their pet, this is a learning session. Dogs learn a great deal about us by our body language, something we are rarely aware of. Particular actions will be preceded by certain behaviour and dogs learn from this as quickly as from thought-out training methods. Your Bernese puppy will learn bad habits and undesirable reactions as easily as he will learn desired behaviour, so careful thought must be given to his future development.

Bernese are best trained through guidance rather than force. Bad habits can be undone, but a considerable amount of time and effort is needed. Many of the Bernese I have re-homed through our Welfare Service have been mis-managed as youngsters, due to a lack of time and training input. It is so sad when owners have to part with a dog because it is badly behaved. Certainly, some puppies are more stubborn than others, and, dare I say, some are more stupid than others. But the Bernese is willing, if not always capable, and this is a good temperament to train. Mistakes will occur and bad habits, to a greater or lesser degree, will be acquired. But how established these habits become is the owner's responsibility. Many years ago when I was learning to be an obedience instructor, I was offered a piece of advice which has served me well. Study closely your dog's behaviour. Note his behaviour both leading up to and following actions which you would rather he did not do. Try to think as he would, and consider all the reasons why he may be doing this, before you offer corrective treatment.

From the day your Bernese arrives, mutual respect must be established. Although loving and willing companions, Bernese need a little space sometimes. You must never allow the puppy to take liberties with you, your family or any person, and likewise he should never be pulled about harshly or disturbed when eating or trying to sleep. Your puppy should never be given reason to resent a person or regard a person as a threat. He should be raised with care and consideration and careful planning. A small, lightweight collar can be worn by a puppy in a one-dog household; boisterous play between two or more dogs can result in injury if collars are worn. Bernese do grow into large dogs and if badly trained, or indeed untrained, they may need a good strong collar and lead for control. However, there is no need for your puppy to wear a heavy collar as he will hopefully be trained with care. Adult Bernese must be responsive to the guidance of the lead and collar. This is best achieved by choosing the best equipment to suit your particular dog, not just buying what other large-breed dogs may wear. For a puppy I like to use a thin, lightweight collar, something similar to what a cat may wear, although obviously much longer. It is easy to teach a youngster to respect the lead, and you can then graduate to a thicker or heavier collar as your pet grows. A large, heavy collar or chain will make the neck of a puppy insensitive, and just accustom him to discomfort around his neck. Weight for weight, a dog is stronger than a person; he is able to put all the force of his chest and the thrust of his hindquarters to pull against his collar and lead, if allowed. The trick of owning a pet that walks nicely and responds to guidance from the lead, is to start young with the correct aids.

As soon as the puppy arrives, his future behaviour can begin to be moulded. The most important thing for a Bernese to learn is to always sit before he receives any fuss or attention. The whole problem of over-excitement can be avoided by insisting on this before he learns otherwise. It is very simple to push his rump firmly down into the sit position whenever he comes for a stroke, at feeding time or when greeting visitors. Later on he will do this naturally, making it easier to put on a lead for walks, and waiting to get in and out of the car. Bernese can be clumsy and some do jump up, so again this simple routine for attention will avoid visitors being buried under a great hairy dog when they arrive! Some owners who wish to show their dog, will not want a pet who sits at every opportunity, but Bernese will learn the command to stand, just as easily. All puppies are great chewers: and the problem of finger-chewing is lessened if the puppy is sitting down being fussed, rather than darting back and forth while trying to grab fingers.

Most owners want a pet which will be calm and steady, and inherited temperament allowing, this is easily achieved. Never, never encourage rough play-fighting with your pet from the children or anyone else. Puppies, like children, can become over-excited during play, so look for the warning signals and put a stop to hyper-activity. A Bernese puppy can also get rather grumpy, especially with children who insist on annoying him when he is trying to sleep. Avoid these occurrences and you will rarely have a problem. Visitors to your home will, no doubt, be enchanted by the new member of your family. But beware, visitors take great delight in teaching naughty habits. Surprisingly, a bad habit encouraged by a visitor becomes ingrained far more quickly than the good habits you are trying to teach. Even though you cannot devote every moment to your pet, don't let him misbehave when you are entertaining visitors. If you remove him from the room, he will just amuse himself until he is allowed in again. A firm grip of the situation must be taken to ensure good manners in the future.

A wire crate or a small wired-off area is esential for initial training. The puppy has all-round vision, but is confined so he cannot be a nuisance or get into mischief while his owner is otherwise engaged. A large crate would be needed to enable the puppy to move about easily. I have also heard many reports of quick toilet training by using a crate, as puppies do not like to soil their bed and will try to hold themselves until owners take them outside to perform. Used wisely, a crate can be of great benefit during training, but it is not an essential requisite. House training can take a long time unless extra vigilance is maintained. It is no use putting the puppy outside and expecting him to perform. Sometimes he will and sometimes he won't. But even if he does he will not have learned anything, unless he has been accompanied and praised and so understands what is expected of him.

During the first few weeks in his new home, the puppy's experiences will be limited to happenings within your home, or maybe short trips in the car. Use this time wisely: there is plenty of time to worry about his behaviour away from home once he has completed his vaccination programme. A close bond between puppy and owner is achieved through love and attention. Bernese love to sit with people, and owners who talk gently to their puppy definitely get a strong relationship with their dogs. It doesn't matter whether he understands what you are saying or not: Bernese just adore to be part of what is happening, and the more time you can spend with your puppy, the easier it will be to get him through these first few formative months. If your Bernese puppy is to live with other pets, he must learn respect and to take his place in the pecking order. An established older dog may well rebuff the puppy's attentions, and this will be accepted with better results than if you chastise the puppy yourself. Older dogs rarely want to hurt a puppy, but a firm growl or sharp snap will certainly take the edge off the puppy's impudence. Some older dogs will tolerate any amount of teasing from a puppy, and if this happens, then it is up to you as the owner to step in. Cats can react to a new puppy in a number of ways, but they are always capable of looking after themselves. It is unlikely that the puppy will be clawed in the eye, which is the common owner worry, and certainly a sharp rebuff from the front end of a cat will be far better remembered than your verbal warnings. Short, sharp shock treatment from older established pets is the natural way to teach your puppy his place. Introduction to smaller pets or livestock should also be made as soon as possible, so that the puppy regards these things as normal and learns to accept them without great excitement.

A very important aspect of training is teaching the puppy to be groomed and examined without a struggle. Regular grooming will be a way of life for a pet and he should learn to accept this happily. A regular check of teeth, toes and ears can be undertaken more easily if the puppy learns to be still during the procedure. To your Bernese, you are the master and so he should never try to avoid your attentions. During car trips, be sure to take someone with you so that if the puppy misbehaves, there is someone to correct him while you drive. If he is to travel in the rear of an estate car, he will never need to be put behind a car guard if he has received ample tuition. For safety and peace of mind, he should be encouraged to sit still and look out of the windows, or maybe he could be given a treat – perhaps a bone or chew – to keep him occupied, but above all still! The means by which you get the desired reaction are not so important as the action itself. If he is to travel in a saloon car, then the rear seat is the place to be, and again he should be accompanied by a second person, who can keep him still and under control. As your puppy grows older, he may begin to move about more in the car and this should be corrected immediately. Barking in the car is extremely dangerous, as it can distract the driver. At dog shows, I am often amazed at the noise coming from excited dogs in cars. This is a bad habit that must be stopped firmly and immediately. A puppy may bark from the protective interior of a car if he is startled by something. But no matter what the reason, this potentially dangerous habit must be prevented. Puppies will bark during play and this is quite normal. Some owners may like their Bernese to speak on command – indeed this is a requirement of some obedience tests. But barking should not be allowed to become a habit. Noisy dogs are a real nuisance and you will not be popular with your neighbours if you allow unnecessary barking.

Puppies usually settle into a new home easily, though it will take a little time for both of you to get used to each other's ways and habits. Planning future training may be too much to deal with initially, but the sooner you decide what is and is not allowed, the better. What may appear cute in a fat baby puppy may not evoke the same reaction when a large, heavy adult behaves in the same way. You will both be happier if the puppy functions within certain boundaries, so plan his future as surely as you would that of a newborn child.

It is vital that your Bernese puppy receives a full course of vaccinations against the contagious canine diseases. Your local veterinary surgeon will advise at what age the first of the two-part inoculation programme should be given. Your puppy should stay within the boundaries of your own home and garden until advised by the vet. It is impossible to protect him against every germ which he may come into contact with, but it is false economy to fail to give him the protection which modern science and knowledge can offer. Usually, the puppy will be covered approximately ten days after the second inoculation, and then you can take him out to socialise him and continue his education.

LEAD TRAINING

It is possible to familiarise your puppy with his lead and collar within the confines of your garden, so that he will know how to follow you outside. Some puppies will accept the lead quite happily, with just a little persuasion. A little care and plenty of patience are all that is needed to teach him to accept this new activity, although I know that some owners have encountered difficulties when their Bernese have misunderstood the lead to be a terrible punishment. Force should never be used if you want to avoid upsetting your puppy, and remember that Bernese are sensitive and are easily distressed when young. If you have not been able to teach your puppy to accept the lead before he is allowed out, then perhaps the following method will bring about the desired reaction. I like to carry or drive my puppy to a quiet spot, a park or field where there are few distractions. Choose a quiet time of day, when children are at school and no passers-by will interfere. Walk out into the middle of the open space and put the puppy on the ground. Most Bernese will just sit for a moment, surveying the unfamiliar surroundings and marvelling at the big wide world. The lead and collar should have already been put on, but left trailing behind the puppy. As soon as your puppy seems happy about his surroundings, walk off slowly, calling him and encouraging him to follow. If he fails to follow, then take time and just move a few paces away and maybe sit on the grass, talking quietly to him and reassuring him. Once he is mobile you can feel very pleased with yourself, as the rest of the exercise is easy. Even the boldest Bernese puppy will keep fairly close to you as you are the only familiar thing in sight, and the bond already built over the past few weeks makes you the alpha member of the pack, the one to be followed. Don't be tempted to pick up the lead at this stage; just be content to walk, quietly encouraging the puppy to follow you. At a suitable spot, pick up the puppy and return. Repeat this same pattern once or twice more before going further or picking up the lead.

The first lesson that your Bernese will have learned is that it is quite natural to stay close to you when you are outside. It is much better that he should follow you because of his insecurity, than to be pulled and jolted along, which could spoil him. The easy progression from the pattern already set, is to pick up the lead, and most Bernese will hardly notice this, as they have already accepted that it is correct to follow you. All too often, novice owners take great pains to lead-train the puppy, teaching him that the outside world holds no fears. Only later do they let the puppy loose to run free. By this time, he is so confident that you are soon forgotten as he investigates every sight and smell. Clever owners will make good use of young Bernese's insecurity and their reactions when in unfamiliar surroundings to gain the desired response. Confidence can be built up later, so make good use of opportunities as they present themselves when teaching your Bernese new things.

Young Bernese do not need very much organised exercise, but a puppy should certainly be taken out and about as much as possible between resting periods. The more situations he is introduced to, the more he will accept happily. Take him to the shops and just stand quietly in a suitable place so that he can watch the comings and goings of shoppers and traffic without feeling threatened or over-awed. There is no point in trying to walk the puppy along for any distance in such a busy situation, as his mind will be distracted in too many directions. It is wiser to accustom him to all the sights and sounds, and do your lead-training in a quiet situation. Socialisation outings take a great deal of energy on the part of the puppy, even if he is only sitting watching the world go by, so adequate rest following these outings must be allowed.

I wholeheartedly recommend owners to enrol their Bernese for a basic obedience course; even experienced owners can make use of the classes to teach the puppy how to react when in the presence of other dogs and people. Inexperienced owners will quickly appreciate the benefit of working with a Bernese at training classes, and a few hours spent on this kind of education is well worth the effort, as the benefits will be reaped during the rest of your Bernese's life.

Training a dog, any dog, is more a matter of owner attitude than owner experience. Bernese can be the easiest breed in the world, and many owners have reported how their dogs have seemed to know instinctively how to behave with little or no correction. But many of the Bernese I have seen put up for re-homing have been mismanaged, usually by lack of time spent on education, and these have been difficult to rehabilitate. Old habits die hard in dogs as well as people. Training your Bernese is a commitment, and consistent commands and guidance will bring the best results.

CHAPTER EIGHT

General Care and Management

SLOW to mature but fast to grow, Bernese need careful management for the first twelve to eighteen months if they are to grow into fit, healthy, beautiful representatives of the breed. Starting from around a pound in weight at birth and growing to well over a hundred pounds on maturity for a male, it is not surprising that problems can and do occur. Hereditary defects do appear in some Bernese, but there is no doubt that the effect upon the dog can be enhanced or minimised by feeding, exercise and general management. Bernese from different family groups or bloodlines grow and develop at different rates, and so breeders should always be approached for advice in the first instance. What may be right for one Bernese, may be detrimental for another.

Exercise, how much and how often, is a much debated subject in point. A true working dog, the Bernese should be able to do as much or as little as their original job required of them. Bred as a general purpose farm dog, we can assume that the daily tasks for such a dog would vary from day to day, and season to season. My own belief is that a Bernese adult should be capable of activity all day if needed, and have the stamina to earn his living. But he should not be so highly strung that he needs to be exhausted each day in order to behave tolerably. Bernese puppies are rather heavy for their size and so great care should be taken not to overtax them or create too much stress on their soft skeleton. For the first three and a half months of life, a Bernese will get all the exercise he needs from his daily activities within the confines of his home and garden. He will be able to rest and sleep as he feels the need, and days of high activity will be compensated for by extra rest the next day. In their enthusiasm to educate a newly vaccinated Bernese, some owners forget that the initial outings of a puppy are for education and socialisation, not exercise. During organised walks, a puppy is unable to tell you when he has had enough, and indeed his Bernese temperament will encourage him to follow you, even when he feels exhausted. Organised exercise periods should, therefore, be kept short, and increased very gradually during the first six months of life.

A three-and-a-half-month old puppy, once accustomed to the lead, can be walked at a steady pace for about ten minutes once a day, increasing to twice daily within three or four weeks. This is in addition to his free exercise at home. A happy balance must be found: enough exercise and activity to help muscle and co-ordination development, yet not too much resulting in fatigue and skeletal stress. The food consumed by your puppy should be used for maintenance and growth, but all too often over-exercise burns up some of the food which should be used for growth. Free running is more tiring to your puppy than a steady walking or trotting pace, which will help to get the body moving together smoothly. From four-and-a-half to around six-months-old, controlled walks can be increased gradually in both time and frequency: twenty to thirty minutes at a time, once or twice a day, or perhaps more activity at weekends with compensating rest following. Bernese grow in an uneven way: slow growth periods interspersed with rapid growth spurts. Exercise will need to be flexible to fit in with the growth rates, and controlled exercise rather than marathon galloping sessions is advisable. Extra care must also be taken to ensure that playtimes with other dogs are not too boisterous, so risking injury.

From six to nine-months-old, a routine will be emerging, although flexibility is still necessary. Some owners will be showing their puppies, and if so, I would recommend that the puppy is allowed to rest completely for the whole day following a show outing. Freedom to come and go in the garden will be more than enough after such a tiring day. If several shows are on the agenda, limit daily walks to compensate for this extra stress, just keeping enough rhythmic walking to maintain muscle control and help further co-ordination. Bernese do not finish growing, height wise, until about fifteen or sixteen-months-old. From about one year, many owners regard their dog as adult, but really a Bernese should still be treated as a puppy, at that age. Males especially go through some surprising teenage stages and exercise should be limited in order to counteract the frequent lack of condition experienced by these adolescents.

The amount of exercise offered to an adult depends upon your family situation, as well as the temperament of your dog. All dogs love to go out and free run and see new sights and sounds. But the exercise regime should always be dictated by you and not the dog. If your lifestyle enables you to enjoy a lot of exercise with your Bernese, that is fine. But if the routine changes do not expect your dog to accept it without protest. With increased exercise your dog will not only become fit, he will gain stamina which in turn, enables him to do more exercise. Owners of hyperactive Bernese often make the mistake of increasing exercise in an effort to tire the dog, so making him easier and more settled to live with. Nothing could be further from the truth. If an over-active Bernese is your reason for giving lots of exercise, then a complete change of attitude is the only way to bring about a change in the daily activity level of your pet. At the opposite end of the scale, we sometimes see Bernese which are very lazy, and reluctant to take exercise unless encouraged. This is really not the correct attitude for a working dog, and so a regular routine should be undertaken for fitness.

Working Bernese, whether they are involved in farm, obedience or rescue work, will need extra food for the increased energy output. As long as your Bernese is well and happy, then an adult can do as much exercise as both you and he feels happy with. If his general condition is good, then you can continue. Exercise should always be increased slowly, whether you have a young or an older dog. But generally, old Bernese will not want the amount of activity they enjoyed when younger. Even so, old dogs should be taken out at regular intervals to keep their bodies functioning well. I am sure that many premature deaths are caused by lack of fitness.

In recent years, with the problems of hip dysplasia and osteochondritis dissecans gaining prominence in canine and scientific publications, some owners have attributed good conformation to giving lots of exercise. Whether this is true or not I cannot say: I can only speak from my own and from friends' experiences. Certainly, taking exercise with your Bernese is a most enjoyable way to spend time in his company, and this helps to keep both of you well. Physical stimulation certainly improves mental activity, and so from that point of view alone, exercise is a necessity. Bernese which are to be shown will need to be fit with good muscle tone, but most show Bernese are improved in outline if they carry a few more pounds of bodyweight than their working counterparts. Whatever the future holds for your pet, the exercise routine must be consistent in order to maintain his best condition.

GROOMING

Grooming your Bernese should be a regular and enjoyable experience for both you and your dog. The routine will change as the puppy coat changes to adult coat, and at certain casting times more grooming is needed to keep your pet happy and comfortable. Regular grooming sessions will also enable you to examine your pet for parasites, lumps, cuts and abrasions. Grooming will enable you to familiarise yourself with your pet's body and any changes will be recognised and advice can be sought quickly.

The correct equipment will make the job easier than merely making do with any old brush and comb that may be about. There are vast arrays of grooming equipment on show in pet shops and the novice owner may be confused by this. The two most essential items are a metal comb, with both wide and narrowly spaced teeth, and a slicker brush. It is well worth buying the best that you can afford, even though cheaper items are available. Good quality grooming tools will last the lifetime of your Bernese and they are made for efficiency; less expensive items are usually less durable. A comb with a handle is more comfortable for the user than one with teeth running all the way along the spine. So often owners do not consider their own comfort, and consequently grooming sessions become unattractive with tools that are awkward to handle. Be sure to hold the comb in your hand for a few minutes to see how comfortable it feels as it warms from your body temperature. The teeth of the comb should be carefully inspected to make sure that they are smooth and well-rounded at the tip. Inexpensive combs sometimes have jagged edges to the teeth where the metal has been clumsily coated. Nickel-coated combs may look shiny and bright, but stainless steel is by far the best for quality long-term. Slicker brushes look like flat pads inset with a collection of wire rakes. This kind of brush is ideal for both puppy and adult coats, but it does have to be used with care. During coat-casting, it is the best thing for taking out dead coat, and at other times it will quickly separate the hairs of the coat to give a smart appearance without too much effort. Slicker brushes come in a number of sizes and shapes: and so again, look at the quality and workmanship before buying. I have found a large, curved slicker brush to be the most valuable tool of all, as the shape enables it to be used right down at the root of the hair without scratching the dog's skin.

Young Bernese puppies tend to have a rather woolly and dense coat which acts as a magnet to dirt and dust. Sometimes, the dense nature of the hair prevents the circulation of air reaching the skin, and dandruff or scurfiness is often present. The slicker brush, if used too harshly, can bring this to the surface, but the brush is not the cause of the problem: it is merely bringing it to light. Grooming a Bernese is most easily achieved with the dog on a table or on a raised platform. If taught early, this will be accepted by your Bernese, who will be only too delighted to have your full attention during these times. A puppy is less likely to wriggle about if he is raised from the floor, and owners are not subject to back-aches or sore knees from prolonged kneeling.

GROOMING A PUPPY
The woolly puppy coat really needs to be groomed every day, not only to remove the dirt collected during his explorations, but also to encourage the new adult coat to come through. Regular grooming is very beneficial to the skin and has a massaging effect, encouraging the natural oils to be evenly distributed. A puppy coat is rarely shiny until the new adult coat starts to appear, but the condition of the hair will be much improved by regular and thorough grooming.

Start by sitting the puppy on your table or platform, making sure that he is well under control and not able to jump or fall off and injure himself. Bernese are usually more than happy to relax while being brushed, but do not take chances with puppies. Talk to the pup gently, reassuring him, and start with the chest so that he can see what you are up to. I like to use the comb here: a combination of long- and short-toothed comb if he has collected a lot of dirt since the previous session; the narrow-tooth comb if he looks fairly clean. Start up under the armpits and work down the tummy as far as you can see. Then go back to the starting point and comb a band at a time, moving higher as each level is combed through until you reach the throat area.

I then move to the back of the head, and again using both types of comb I work down the neck, being careful not to pull the hair or snag the skin. Longer coats should be groomed from the rear end, forward in bands. But a puppy coat can be combed with the lie of the hair until the puppy is about three-and-a-half to four-months-old. From the back of the neck, comb down through the shoulder area, linking up with the groomed chest. Special attention should be paid to the rather fine hair around the ears, and the narrow-spaced comb is best employed here. The body can be combed through a section at a time, taking care to check the skin for abrasions or signs of parasites as you go. Most puppies will sit or lie quite happily, but many will show interest when you reach the tail. Why this is, I do not know, but a firm hold is usually needed until he becomes accustomed to the procedure. The hair under the tail – the tan-coloured anal patch – should be combed downwards, towards the hock. Take care not to catch the tendon that runs down the back of his hind leg with the comb.

Once the coat has been combed through, a gentle going-over with the slicker brush will ensure that any loose hairs are removed and any dust lifted. The legs and under-belly should be combed with the narrow-spaced end of the comb. If the hair is tangled or you find dried-on dirt, resist the temptation to pull the comb through, ripping out the tangle and the attached hair. Your Bernese will resent grooming sessions if he experiences pain, so take time to ease problem patches out gently, a little at a time. I like to comb the leg hair and featherings upwards – the wrong way – as it is very close-lying here and combing along its natural direction doesn't always allow the dirt and dust to escape. The hair on the hocks takes a lot of battering from day to day. It comes into contact with the ground every time the puppy sits or lies down, and so can easily become soiled. Owners who plan to show, like to train this hair to stand out from the hock, rather than allowing it to lie naturally, to give the impression of heavier bone in the show ring.

Once you are satisfied that the coat has been well separated, then a general inspection should follow. The ear flaps on a puppy can collect dirt or appear a little greasy. Many ear cleaning preparations are available from pet shops: if these are gently wiped on and then removed with cotton wool, it will avoid future problems. If dirt or discharge is present in the ear canal, it should be removed with a cotton bud. Only wipe away what can be easily seen; do not probe down into the ear, but seek expert advice if mites are present. Any greasy or waxy deposits can be removed with just warm water if a preparatory cleaner is not available. Benzyl benzoate, used warm in a one part to two of water, is very good and will not cause irritation if used to removed more stubborn dirt. Surgical or methylated spirit in a one part to four of water mixture can also be used. After cleaning, the ear should be dried with cotton wool.

Bernese eyes are usually bright and clean, but they should always be checked for irritation. If the eyes appear a little crusty, gently wipe away dry flakes around the eye with a damp sponge. Cotton wool or absorbent paper should be avoided as they will break up when wet and possibly leave particles in the eye.

Nails on puppies can be rather sharp, even though an adult Bernese has short, well-managed nails. Experienced owners can easily cut the nails with a good strong pair of nail clippers; the pincer type are far more efficient than the guillotine kind. The toe nails can be clear or dark pigmented, and great care should be taken not to cut them so short as to slice through the quick. If a puppy's nails are very sharp, then just the point should be removed. Inexperienced owners should seek advice from the vet or an experienced breeder before risking damaging the puppy through ignorance. Once shown, owners can shorten nails in future. Filing of nails is practised by some owners and, although this is efficient, it is rather time-consuming, and may be rather frightening for a young puppy. As your puppy grows, his nails will be naturally shortened by contact with the ground. This does not apply to the dew claw on the front legs, and if this has not been removed at birth it will need to be checked regularly. Dew claws can grow round and penetrate the leg if neglected.

Look between the toes and underneath between the pads as small stones and grit can cause soreness, and thorns can bring about abscesses. If redness is present, I would advise that some of the hair be carefully cut away from under the foot and between the toes, and then the foot can be washed and dried more easily to allow efficient treatment.

Puppies should have their teeth inspected, especially during teething, to ensure that everything is coming along as expected. Infant canines are sometimes retained after the adult canines have appeared, and under or overshot bites can cause some teeth to penetrate to the gums or the roof of the mouth. Gentle mouth examination will soon be happily accepted by a puppy, and I have to admit, I reward my own puppies with a titbit after grooming and examination sessions. As your Bernese puppy grows, you should decide what position you prefer him to be in during grooming. I like my adults to lie flat out on their sides and I finish the session with them standing. Others may prefer them to stand from the start. At shows, I have often seen dogs being given a thorough grooming, and if this is the routine for you, then your dog must obviously be taught to stand. But I believe that Bernese should always be groomed at home before a show and they will only need a tidying-up on arrival.

Once the adult coat has appeared on your Bernese, the grooming routine will change slightly. An older puppy or adult will not collect so much dirt from daily activities, but as the coat is longer it may still become matted. The wide-tooth comb is the first tool to use, and I start from the bottom of the chest, working up in bands as before. Then, I start at the root of the tail and comb through sections, combing along the natural lie of the hair, but working toward the dog's head. When this procedure is complete, I do the same with a narrow-spaced comb, finishing up with the slicker brush, which will help the coat to lie naturally and comfortably. Ear, eye, mouth and feet checks are also wise to ensure that your pet is well. The hair around the ears will grow into long streamers if allowed, and easily forms tangles and matts. It is very common for this area to be neglected, and many apparently well-groomed dogs are found to have large matted tags on close inspection. Pet owners sometimes cut away some of the long hair, but this must be a personal decision.

The featherings at the back of the front legs and around the trouser area of the hind legs can be rather coarse and dry. This can also become clogged, and so extra attention is needed. Adults grow very long hair between the pads, and the underside of the feet can become very matted. You would think that this hair would give the dog natural protection, but I have always found it is more likely to attract problems, so I cut it away. Dogs sweat through their pads and so this will help to make them more comfortable. On a practical level, it also stops a lot of dirt and mud being brought into the house. A tag of matted hair will also appear between the second and third toes on both the front and hind feet and this will certainly cause soreness if left. It is difficult to groom between the actual toes, so any clogging should be simply cut away.

The sexual organs of adults should be checked regularly to ensure that all is well. Many males have a slight discharge from the sheath; this is quite normal and usually troublefree. The creamy-coloured deposit can dry and clog and so it can be gently combed away. Excess hair growth here may be trimmed to make for easier cleaning, as urine drips can cause a smell if allowed to collect and dry. The area around the vulva of a bitch can also become clogged from natural secretions, and this too can be trimmed if necessary. Small cysts or sore spots can appear on the vagina. This is caused by urine which is too acid, cystitis or other infections. These are all easily dealt with, if prompt advice is sought. Experienced owners may wish to empty the anal glands of their Bernese, but novices should certainly go to the vet if they suspect that their Bernese needs help to evacuate these glands. Bernese, which usually accept examination happily, can become rather concerned if you pay attention to the area under the tail, so indicating a possible problem. Anal glands that are left unchecked, can cause severe discomfort to the dog if they become full, or impacted.

The condition of your Bernese's coat and skin is a product not only of the grooming routine, but of feeding. A dry, dull coat may be caused by inadequate grooming, but it may also be connected to hormone imbalance or insufficient nutrition. Overall good condition starts inside the dog, and no amount of grooming can improve a coat if adequate nourishment is lacking.

Moulting

Entire adults – those not neutered – moult on a fairly regular cycle, although abrupt changes in the weather can bring about coat-casting or indeed growth. Bitches moult twice a year, usually before a season, although they have a more severe cast after having a litter of puppies. Dogs usually moult once yearly, and mature males may hold a coat much longer as they get older. It is usual to get some hair from the dog at each grooming session, but once the moult proper begins, then more attention will prevent the hair from being deposited all over the house.

The first sign of coat-casting is usually a dullness to the coat. Small tufts of hair will be

Before a moult.

combed out rather than the odd hairs previously seen. If neglected, large clumps will rise to the surface and this undercoat needs to be quickly removed otherwise uncomfortable mats and tags will form. Retention of dead coat will inhibit the emergence of the new growth, and if air cannot circulate freely then the risk of skin irritation and insect or parasite infestation is increased. The moult can last for about three weeks or can continue for a good deal longer. But you can feel a sense of relief when the coat left on your Bernese feels rather more harsh than normal. This is brought about by the lack of soft, cushioning undercoat and heralds the end of the shedding process. Because Bernese are a solid-looking breed, owners may fall into the misconception of thinking that their Bernese is rather thin when he has moulted. Lack of undercoat can make him appear to be rather slimmer than normal. But do not increase the amount of food offered unless you are sure that he needs it, and is not merely looking lean through lack of coat. Bathing or swimming will increase the speed at which dead hair is shed. Two or three baths at weekly intervals will be most beneficial to both your Bernese and the vacuum cleaner!

UNUSUAL COATS
The coat of the Bernese can vary from dog to dog, even incorporating some coat types which are undesired in breed terms. Not all Bernese are typical but even so, they are loved by their owners and need the same care and attention as those with more correct coats.

After a moult.

Curly coats are deemed attractive by some owners, but they certainly need more care than coats without this fault. Loose hair tends to be retained and so matting and clogging is a regular occurrence. When a slicker brush is used on a curly coat it will cause some hair to be torn out as it curls around the wire rakes. A very wide-toothed comb followed by a narrow-toothed comb are best applied in that order. Dirt and dust is more readily trapped, so extra grooming attention is needed to keep your Bernese happy. Smooth coats, those which are very short, also appear sometimes. These are easier to deal with, but some owners are tempted to neglect grooming because the coat seems so easy to manage.

Neutered males and females can experience definite changes in coat length, texture, density and condition. My experience has been that a few months after spaying or castration, Bernese suffer a more severe moult than ever previously seen. Once the new coat grows in, it will be retained better, and moults will be less frequent than when the dog was entire. Some males and females will grow a coat as normal, but many will gain increased length and density. Heavy undercoats can appear, and much more grooming is necessary to prevent the coat from getting out of control. Extra long hair is seen on the featherings and tail, and this may need to be trimmed for ease of maintenance. A rather dry, woolly effect can also be experienced and this really does need careful management. The skin can appear rather drier than before neutering, but in many cases a greasiness will be noticed. This condition lends itself to matting dead hair very easily. Extra hair growth can be trimmed if desired, but the most important point is to ensure that your Bernese, especially if he is rather old, does not become overheated in hot weather due to his thicker jacket.

BATHING

It is rather old-fashioned to accept the recommendation that dogs should not be bathed as it removes natural oils from their coats. This really is nonsense. A dirty Bernese will be much happier after a good wash and he is a much more acceptable part of the family if clean. All dogs get dusty, dirty and wet and they need a good clean-up from time to time. Show dogs get bathed before every show and, far from suffering any ill effects, their coats are usually in superb, shining form. Pet dogs can be bathed as often as each owner desires. I know some dogs which have never been bathed in their lives. They have not suffered, but they were a bit smelly. A lot of dirt and mud will drop out of the coat when dry, but nevertheless, I think that a bath at least twice a year is about the minimum for a Bernese. Regular use of anti-parasite sprays can build up on the coat, and the residue should not be left to accumulate.

The type of shampoo used can vary, depending on how you want the dog to look and smell. As in shampoos made for people, there are literally hundreds of brands all claiming to do something more wonderful than the other manufacturers' products. Some canine shampoos are more harsh than others and some may be insecticidal. Coloured shampoos are available, but if the dog is to be shown, then these should be avoided as they may leave traces of pigment on the coat which could lead to disqualification.

I prefer not to use insecticidal shampoos for puppies as I feel that they are a bit harsh for a sensitive skin. A simple, no-fuss preparation as recommended by other owners is usually a safe buy. Shampoos which contain added oils and conditioners can leave the coat full of static electricity which in turn attracts dirt and dust, and so you are back to square one. A human frequent-use or baby shampoo is useful in an emergency, but harsh detergents or even washing-up liquid should never be used. For adults, a careful choice of product is still essential, even though a sensitive skin is not so apparent. Many owners use an anti-dandruff preparation and these can be excellent at clearing scurf when used regularly.

It doesn't really matter where you choose to bathe your Bernese, as long as you take enough time over the task. A very young puppy can be washed in a sink, but as he grows this is not possible. A larger puppy can be sat in a shower tray, placed in your own bath or one outside, or even showered under a hosepipe. Whichever way you choose, plenty of warm water will be needed. It is not essential for the dog to stand in water, as in a bath, but a few inches of water will help to wet him initially. I have found that by washing my dogs in the bath or shower, most of the drying can be done in the same place, so mess is minimal. If you must do the job outside, then a shower attachment is essential to ensure that the water is the right temperature. Cold water should never be used to rinse the dog, as apart from being a shock to his system, it will not rid the coat of all the shampoo residue. Many owners fail to rinse their dog thoroughly, and this is one of the reasons why so many dogs look dull after a bath: the coat is not completely clean.

Before you get the dog for his bath, ensure that you have everything that you need assembled within easy reach. A non-slip rubber mat should be put in the bath or shower tray to prevent the dog from slipping. Bernese don't usually struggle but they are very clumsy and could easily be frightened. The shampoo should be diluted with water, as it is much easier to use than when applied as a thick gel. I have found that instead of towels, the synthetic chamois leathers made for drying wet dogs are super for the job, as they are much more absorbent than towelling and wring out to be used time and time again. Your Bernese should be well groomed and free from dead hair before he is bathed; tangles will result if he is washed while carrying loose hair. All matts should have been removed and any excess hair should have been trimmed away so you only wash what you want to keep. Leather collars should not be worn in the bath, as the dye will stain the white area under his chin and around his neck. A lightweight webbing collar is ideal for control and will not hinder the operation. It is a good idea for the owner or washer to wear a waterproof apron or, if one is not available, a plastic refuse-sack held in place with a belt will suffice.

Once the dog is in the bath or shower, the water can be either poured over your Bernese with a jug, or ideally sprayed on with a shower attachment. The temperature of the water must be carefully gauged, neither too hot nor too cold. Always keep your hand on the dog's coat where the water is applied, to prevent the dog being scalded. In homes where the plumbing system is rather out of date, ensure that the water isn't turned on in another room by a member of the family: your Bernese may get a shock if the water temperature suddenly changes as the water is drawn elsewhere. It will take at least five to ten minutes to ensure that a full-grown Bernese is wet right down to the skin, and some dirt will be rinsed away during this process. Only when the dog is thoroughly wet should the shampoo be applied. I like to rub it to a lather on the white parts first, leaving it to do its work while I am attending to the rest of the coat. If the diluted shampoo is applied from a redundant washing up liquid bottle, then it will go exactly where it is wanted with little or no waste. Lather up a small area of the body at a time, leaving the legs until last. Special attention can be given to the under-belly and inside the thighs: these areas are often forgotten, but a lot of grime collects here. Once your Bernese is fully lathered, rinse him well until the water runs clear, and repeat the process. Two applications are necessary to remove all the dirt, although less shampoo is needed for the second soaping. I see no reason in doing the job at all unless it is going to be done properly. There are few things that make you more proud than admiring your newly bathed Bernese in all his splendour.

The final rinse is the all-important part. Apart from keeping the shampoo well away from the dog's eyes and ear canals, the rinsing water should also be kept from other sensitive areas. The muzzle, if dirty, is best cleaned by rubbing with a damp cloth, rather than trying to rinse with the spray. Fifteen to twenty minutes is the minimum time needed to rinse your Bernese thoroughly, and quite probably it will take longer. The water should be sprayed on while your other hand is rubbing the coat, encouraging the lather to surface. When rinsing in the same direction as the lie of the coat, it is easy to be fooled that the soap has all gone, only to find large areas of soap when you are trying to dry the dog. The rinsing water should be allowed to flow away as it is applied, as it is of no use a second time through the coat.

Once you are sure that the coat is clear of shampoo, don't be in too much of a hurry to get the dog out of the bath. Blot him dry with your synthetic chamois leather or towels, and keep him where he is until there are no more signs of dripping water. A good ten to fifteen minutes spent here will save a lot of mess as you transfer the dog outside. If you have bathed him in your own bath, do not attempt to clean up the hairs, which are undoubtedly attached to every surface, until they are dry; a clean, dry cloth will be all that is needed to wipe them away. The question of drying depends on the dog, and the weather. Fit, healthy adults will dry quickly in the sun, especially if they are taken for a free run after the bath. But beware that he doesn't roll in something unmentionable, to put back some doggy perfume!

I think that puppies should always be fully dried with a hot-air drier, and this is a relatively quick task. The coat can be gently combed in the stream of hot air, and the puppy will learn to accept the drier if taught young enough. Your hand should always be between the hot air and the dog's skin, to ensure that he doesn't get burned. Your hand can also separate the hair, allowing the air current to be more effective. Old dogs should also be dried, as their joints can become painful if they are left damp for a long time. Once dry, your adult or puppy can be thoroughly groomed, and sprayed with a parasite-repellent.

HOUSING

Before proceeding, I had better admit that I am anti-kennels for Bernese. I accept that it is no hardship for a dog to sleep in a kennel: he will, after all, just be sleeping. On a nice day, a Bernese will probably prefer to lie outside in a run, when left during his owner's absence, rather than be shut indoors where he will see little to interest him. My main dislike of kennel accommodation is that, once provided, many owners use it too often, until the dog is spending more time alone than with the family. A sensible owner attitude is all-important, but so many people find it convenient to simply shut the dog away and forget about him. I will agree, however, that a kennel or outhouse can be useful in a number of ways. On wet days, the dog can dry off before coming into the house, and during family festivities he may well appreciate a place to get a little peace and quiet. Used for short periods, a kennel can be of benefit. For anyone who may plan to breed or keep more than a couple of Bernese, it will be useful when a bitch is in season, or when puppies are big enough to spend some time out of doors playing and running about.

As a general rule, wooden kennels are more easily obtainable than brick or block constructed buildings, unless you have a builder in the family. Permanent structures can be rather cold, although they are more easily disinfected. Wooden buildings can be chewed, and need regular maintenance for continued use. Depending on the planned use, the bigger the kennel, the better. The internal floor space for an adult should not be less than six feet by four feet; enough room is needed for the dog to lie out, and to soil away from his bed if he has an accident.

Buildings should be tall enough for easy cleaning: the crate-sized kennels sometimes seen are of no use at all. A shed-like structure is more useful, with one or more windows for light and ventilation. The sleeping area should be a few inches above ground level to avoid draughts, and the doors should open wide for easy access. A stable-type door is a good idea, and if set well above ground level, a ramp is less dangerous to your dog than steps. Wooden buildings should be well lined and insulation cannot be economised upon. Youngsters may be tempted to chew, especially if left for long periods, so aluminium sheeting can be put around the sides to a height of about two feet. Even brand-new kennels should be treated with a wood preservative, making sure it is not toxic to dogs. A couple of coats of external or marine-grade varnish should be applied to the floor area for easy cleaning and protection.

Brick-built kennels can be rather cold in winter and these also need insulation and possibly protection by means of aluminium sheeting too. Some kind of bedding is needed: a concrete or brick floor is not acceptable for a Bernese, even though they do like to lie in a cool place sometimes. The floor should be slightly higher at the rear than towards the door, so that water will run away after cleaning. Any windows should be covered by a wire grid or some other kind of protection from the feet of a Bernese, although this should not be fixed so the window cannot be opened easily. The door should be placed to one side, if possible, rather than in the centre, so that your Bernese can lie out of the draught if he chooses. I would consider the minimum size of a run for a Bernese to be about ten feet by twenty, and this would be for very short confinements. If all or part of the run can be covered to provide shelter from rain and wind, then it can be employed through inclement weather as well as on fine days. Some Bernese are much more agile than others and some are more inclined to try to find a way out than less worried dogs. The wire around the run should be about six feet high, and a splash-board or small wall around the base of the wire will make cleaning easier and stop hair clogging around the wire set into the ground. The gate should be strong and sturdy and should have a good catch which closes easily. There are few things more annoying than trying to align catches with a Bernese pushing on the gate.

A grass and earth floor to the run is most unsuitable, even though grass does look attractive. It is completely impractical for cleaning. The ground will very quickly become sour and smelly from urine soaking in and, apart from this being offensive, it may also offer a health risk. Paving slabs dry more quickly than solid concrete, but again the urine will soak down between the slabs unless they are completely sealed with a waterproof, non-shrink substance. Solid concrete can take a long time to dry, but is generally more durable in the long term. The run should also be slightly sloping, so that water will run away into a channel and connect up with the drainage system. The surface of the run should be roughened, and this will not only give a good grip, but will help prevent weak pasterns from too flat a surface. Shade from hot sun must be available and a roof on the run may provide this. An overhanging tree will look pretty, but falling leaves will need to be cleared away regularly so as not to block the drain and encourage insects and dampness.

Many kennels become smelly because of the inappropriate use of strong disinfectant liquids. These strong chemicals combine with urine to create a smell just as obnoxious as the one you are trying to remove, and so are best avoided. Pine disinfectant and farm-type cleaners are the worse offenders, and yet are the most often purchased. Good quality household bleach, diluted to the recommended strength, is by far the most effective cleanser. It will neutralise most smells and when rinsed away will leave the run clean and bright and harmless to your pet. If your Bernese has to spend a lot of time in a run, then it should be hosed down at least twice daily. Last thing at night faeces should be removed and urine rinsed away with clean water. Once deposits have gone, a solution of diluted bleach can be brushed well into the base, and when all stains have been removed the residue can be hosed away. The run will then be clean and dry for use next time. In hot weather, faeces should be removed as you notice them, to keep flies to a minimum, and hosing down will help to keep the temperature down for the dog's comfort. In the winter, impacted ice and snow should be removed from the run daily by either hot water or the sprinkling of salt, but great care should be taken to remove all traces of salt which might be irritant to your Bernese. Ample clean drinking water should always be available and this should be placed in the shade and away from falling leaves. Ideally, it should also be placed at the rear of the run to avoid spillage when you are greeted by your dog.

Bedding in your house can be as simple or as luxurious as you please. Your Bernese will be content to lie anywhere as long as he can be near you. Bernese are happy to lie in a cool place, but they do not like to be in a direct draught. A small mat or blanket is ideal for a puppy who may not have too many manners or much respect for his bed. An adult will certainly appreciate something a bit more comfortable. Polystyrene-filled bean-bags are very popular, and greatly treasured by many Bernese. They mould to the shape of the dog, and although warm, they do not make them over-heat. A plastic or wicker basket-type is another option. The plastic type is easier to clean and less of a temptation to chew. Soft bedding, blankets or duvets should be chosen not only for their comfort but also for their ease of washing. A doggy odour will be passed on to bedding, and so regular cleaning is essential. Older Bernese, or those with joint problems, need a comfortable but firm bed on which to lie. Bedding that is too soft is difficult to rise from and will make arthritic joints painful.

FEEDING

There are so many types of prepared foods on the market these days that in a survey of ten people there are bound to be at least seven or eight different foods used. As long as your Bernese gets the correct ratio of vitamins and minerals, proteins and carbohydrates, he is bound to thrive. One of the dangers of feeding a large breed is the risk of bloat or torsion, which can be fatal. Bloat can be brought about by a number of foods, and although many owners worry that complete foods are the cause, a natural diet of meat and meal can also bring about problems.

Owners are often advised to feed high-protein foods, coupled with extra supplementation of calcium to help the heavy skeleton formation of Bernese. It is now accepted in many quarters that a lower protein level is perhaps more desirable, so that growth may be slower but the risk of problems associated with promoted growth will be avoided. Foods too high in protein may also produce hyperactivity. A balanced diet needs no supplementation, unless a diagnosed defect is being treated by supplementation of certain substances. Many of the complete processed diets have a balanced level of nutrients, although different brands vary. The nutritional requirements of a working dog are different to that of a pet that burns off relatively few calories in energy; and a growing dog's needs are different from an adult's. Care should be taken over the choice of food for your Bernese: not only should it suit the individual but it should be consistent in quality, and fit in with the daily routine easily. One dog will do well on one type of food, whereas another will lack condition. Dogs are not like people, they do not need to have a different type of food every day, and I would certainly advise that, if you have a feeding routine which suits both you and your Bernese, you should stay with it.

Bernese are a greedy breed. Very few of them are fussy eaters, and if they are, it is generally the fault of the owners. Mistakes are often made when a new puppy joins a household. In a bid to make the puppy feel at home, he is offered all sorts of foods that he may not have had before. If too many choices are offered, the puppy soon becomes confused and begins to refuse food, until both dog and owner become anxious. At certain times during teething, puppies can become rather fussy for a time, and young males often go through a precarious stage around ten to fourteen months when the feeding pattern may be disrupted. So feeding should be consistent, but common sense should dictate if a change is needed for continued good health.

The traditional diet of fresh meat and good-quality wheatmeal biscuit supplemented with a vitamin and mineral additive seems to be fed by few breeders, although single-dog owners seem to favour this regime. It is easy to think that a meat and biscuit meal is more appetising than a cereal and processed animal-protein diet. But a hungry dog probably doesn't mind either way. There is a real risk that a natural diet may be lacking in one or more nutrients; but if vegetables, various meats and dairy products are also fed, then you can assume that what may be lacking one day will be acquired the next. Of course, a multi-vitamin supplement will avoid such a deficiency. The protein level can be varied easily, to suit your Bernese, by feeding different forms of meat.

Complete, processed foods are often supplemented with some meat to aid palatability, but this is also raising the protein level. Many of these diets are now thought to be rather too high in protein for a Bernese, and indeed there is a school of thought which links these foods with a higher risk of bone deformity. Many owners choose these diets because they *are* complete – so that is how they should be fed. But if this proves unattractive to your Bernese, then feeding meat and meal may be a more advisable option. Another point worth considering is that the faeces from dogs fed on complete foods, especially the cereal type, are often lacking in form, and for the amount consumed there is an increased bulk of waste passed. Tinned meats are always very palatable, but there is a high water content. Some dogs do suffer from diarrhoea when fed tinned meat, but these are few and far between. As a rule, tinned meat would need to be bulked out with a higher proportion of carbohydrate than if fresh meat were offered. Special diets for puppies, nursing mothers, invalids or old dogs must be arranged. Easily digested food should be offered according to taste and physical condition, and the amounts offered at each meal should be small, to avoid overloading the system. Concentrated foods are of great value when feeding a Bernese from one of the above categories. If the appetite is diminished, it is important to ensure that the food which is consumed is highly nutritious.

DIET REQUIREMENTS

WATER:
Water is necessary for life, and a lack of water will bring about death much more quickly than will a lack of any other nutrient. Bernese are, in general, consumers of large quantities of water. An active adult will drink often during the day, no matter what the weather conditions, although obviously more is needed during hot weather or after work. Water is constantly being lost by the body in both urine and faeces waste, and by evaporation from panting. A nursing mother will also lose fluid by the production of milk. Constant access to water is necessary throughout life, and in the nursing of a sick dog, dehydration must be avoided at all costs.

CARBOHYDRATES:
Strictly speaking, carbohydrates are not necessary for a Bernese, but they do form a useful source of energy. Fibre, starch and sugar are forms of carbohydrate and are often found in canine foods, dog biscuit being the commonest way of imparting this nutrient. Starch is found in cereals, but it must be processed in order to be fully digested. Fibre is now recognised as being beneficial to both man and animals, for although it is not digested by

the dog, it does affect the speed at which food passes through the digestive system and can help in cases of constipation. Lactose (milk sugar) is often found to cause diarrhoea in dogs, although this will depend on how much and how often milk is fed.

FAT:

Fat contains about twice the amount of calories compared with a similar weight of carbohydrate or protein, and so is a very good energy-giving source. Dogs are unable to produce the essential fatty acids they need, which must accordingly be provided in their food. Fat also offers the fat-soluble vitamins A, D, E and K, necessary for healthy skin and coat, and reproduction. These essential fatty acids are also known as polyunsaturates. Fat is readily accepted by dogs and serves as an insulating material for the body as well as a store for energy.

MINERALS:

Although needed in only very small amounts, minerals are essential for good health and efficient function. These trace elements are usually provided in adequate amounts from a mixed diet. Most owners are aware that a large breed of dog needs adequate amounts of calcium and phosphorus for healthy bone development, and consequently over-supplementation of these elements is common, with varying results. If you feed vitamin/mineral supplements to your Bernese, be sure to give only the stated amount, as repeated overdosing can be toxic.

PROTEIN:

Two-thirds of the weight of a Bernese consists of water, but the next important constituent of your dog is protein. Since the organs are constantly being repaired and renewed, there is a continual need to take in protein via food. Milk and eggs offer the highest-value protein, followed by fish, meat and offal. Cereal proteins have the lowest value, although soya is equal to meat in terms of use. This does not mean that only meat and dairy products should be fed, but a balance of proteins is essential. Puppies and breeding bitches do need more protein than other classes of dog, but this is usually provided adequately by feeding extra amounts – a higher percentage of protein in the food is not really necessary.

VITAMINS:

Vitamins are needed for regulating body processes, among other things, and are needed in minute amounts. They can be divided into two types. The B group of vitamins are water-soluble and are concerned with the essential digestive and respiratory actions. All, with the exception of B1, are found in sufficient amounts in foods of animal origin. B1 can be found in cereals but it is rendered useless by cooking. The second group of vitamins consists of fat, soluble A, D, E and K, which have already been mentioned. A and D are involved with bone growth and A also helps maintain the mucous membranes and eye-sight. Vitamin A is found in the orange pigment called beta carotin found in carrots and tomatoes. A and D are stored in the body, as are all these groups if fed in excessive amounts. Research has indicated that vitamin E is essential for reproduction and overall muscular condition. Vitamin K should be produced by the dog in adequate quantities and is commonly known as the anti-bleeding vitamin. Vitamins are only needed in minimum amounts, and over-dosing will give no extra benefits: indeed it may be seriously detrimental. Even the large breeds and growing puppies need only a balanced diet with sufficient vitamins; the extras needed for growth come from the extra weight of food consumed. Vitamin supplements should never be fed without veterinary advice.

Many owners find that their Bernese will eat the most unlikely foods. Fruit, sweets, raw vegetables and any number of other things may be consumed with relish. I see no harm in this, as long as these foods are only offered in small amounts. Titbits are given in some households, and often these additions are not allowed for when calculating the amount of food to be given. Once a suitable diet has been found, there is no reason to vary it, if the dog is in good condition. However, regular checks should be given to ensure that your Bernese is not losing condition, and feeding routines should be reassessed regularly to take account of changes in the development of your pet.

When and how often you feed your adult Bernese will depend on many personal factors. When the weather is hot, food may be more readily eaten in the early morning or after dusk, whereas in winter a different routine may be followed. Dogs which are kennelled will burn more energy keeping warm than those which live in the house, so warm meals fed at regular intervals will be beneficial. Many owners like to raise the feeding bowl from the ground as their Bernese gains height: whether this does in fact aid stance I do not know; but it must be more comfortable for the dog to eat, and it seems to prevent some dogs from bolting down their food. A large food dish will fit into the top of a bucket, if a special food bowl stand is thought to be unnecessary. Greedy feeders find it more difficult to bolt food from a large shallow dish than from a deep one, and fast eaters may be slowed by adding a few very large biscuits to the meal. Fine-grade cereals may be more easy to digest, but they do nothing to help eating manners. The dog's digestion is able to cope with most things, but I prefer to watch my dogs chew their food rather than swallow down a soup quickly.

Some owners feel that the dog should not be allowed to drink after a meal, for fear of bloat (gastric torsion). I think that to remove water for more than half a hour could render the dog uncomfortable, especially in hot weather, but the type of food consumed would affect this. Certainly, exercise should not be given for at least an hour, and energetic games should be discouraged until the food has had time to settle in the stomach.

CHAPTER NINE

Working Bernese and Leisure Activities

THE Bernese Mountain Dog still fulfils its original function as a multi-purpose farm dog in its homeland as well as throughout the world. Many fanciers of the breed do not require the Bernese for these tasks, but there is no doubt that a Bernese is happiest working for, and with his master. An intelligent, loyal and steady character make the breed easily adapted to many tasks.

A Bernese's intelligence and love of people make him an ideal choice as a rescue dog on the continent and he has proved his worth here over many years as a trustworthy worker. In Switzerland there are rescue dogs stationed within easy reach of every mountainous area, so they can be mustered quickly in a disaster. Bernese trained in avalanche rescue have also been assigned to help in areas devastated by earthquakes, but extra training is needed to cope with the many different situations and so specially trained dogs are now available for such disasters. Not only are the dogs expected to announce a find of a human body but they also have to be well acquainted with a more hazardous terrain than deep snow. Crumbling buildings, broken glass, explosions and often the absence of efficient artificial light, due to the failure of electricity, are all situations to be encountered.

Ambulance dogs are also used in many parts of the world. Their task is to find injured people, and so anyone walking or standing is automatically ignored as they continue their search. In wooded areas or where visibility is difficult, the dogs are trained to go away from their handlers in a straight line, and to return instantly when called. This ensures that the handler can report to rescue controllers which areas have been thoroughly searched, so allowing the greatest efficiency from the dogs available.

Many kennel clubs and breed clubs organise working and obedience tests which can be enjoyed purely for fun in a very elementary way or pursued as a more serious interest. Working Trials are well suited to a larger breed of dog as the degree of precision needed in obedience is not essential. Companion Dog, Police Dog, Tracking Dog and Utility Dog are all stakes in which to partake in the UK, and similar tests and titles can be worked for in the USA. Agility is a new sport which has become enormously popular throughout the world. It is a timed obstacle course, in which the handler runs around the course with the dog encouraging the dog to successfully negotiate each jump, tunnel, bridge or co-ordination test. Different courses are designed for different sized dogs, and both young and older handlers are catered for. As the Bernese is such a substantial dog, jumping should not be attempted until the dog is fully grown and enjoys perfect health and soundness.

Carting, or to give it its more correct term of Draught Work, is probably second only in popularity to agility in the UK and the USA, although most owners in Switzerland and Germany have either worked or paraded their Bernese in harness. In the UK, decorated cart classes were staged at club shows, and were so popular that working courses were soon devised to enable the dogs to do something more exacting than merely look attractive in stance. Bernese can be introduced to harness at just a few months old, but should never be coupled to a cart or expected to haul any weight until they have completed both bone and muscle development. It probably does no harm to try a young Bernese in a cart at twelve months – but don't be tempted to harness the dog at every opportunity. Bernese usually take to this activity with great ease, they adore being the centre of attention.

The suitability of Bernese as Guide Dogs for the Blind has been investigated in Britain, but only one pure-bred bitch achieved the distinction of serving this way. This was a great landmark in the history of the breed in Britain, and some Bernese cross-breeds were trained for the work. Faster-maturing breeds were generally required for this important task. Therapy dogs have been enlisted in recent years to visit old and infirm people, hospital patients, and those who may benefit from touching and being in the company of a dog. Patients in geriatric homes may have had to leave behind much-loved pets, and the benefits to morale are noticed immediately. Sick patients in hospitals and convalescent homes are lifted by the planned visits of carefully selected dogs and caring owners, and mentally ill patients are noticeably more responsive during and after visits from dogs. The Bernese temperament is certainly ideal for this very useful and rewarding contribution.

This dog visits a hospital regularly to give children rides.   Dickson

CHAPTER TEN

Showing

SHOWING can be described as a sport, a hobby, a pastime or even a way of life, depending on how competitive a person you are. However deeply you decide to become involved, the most important point to remember is that it should always be fun for both you and your dog. If the desire to win becomes too great, you will frequently suffer disappointment, and if misery is the result then perhaps it would be wiser to pursue another interest with your Bernese.

People from many walks of life become enthusiastic about showing and as shows are organised to cater for all tastes, in theory, anyone can plan their 'boundaries'. However, in practice, showing is the kind of hobby which tends to become addictive, and unwary participants may soon find that their lives revolve around the shows. Exhibitors need to have a very special kind of character: the ability to accept victory and defeat with equal grace, a genuine desire to mix with others who share the same interests, good humour, and above all, a real love of the Bernese Mountain Dog, especially your own charges.

Any registered pedigree dog could be exhibited, but only those who represent the breed favourably as laid down in the breed standard should be considered as suitable. Every dog may have his day, as the saying goes, but it is a very sad dog and owner who never seem to achieve success. Showing your Bernese should be regarded as a bonus on top of the enormous pleasure already gained from owning such a wonderful dog, and sometimes we must admit that an individual may not be suitable for this aspect of canine activity. This does not mean that dogs unsuitable for showing can be passed on to allow a more suitable replacement to try its luck. All of us must offer a true commitment to our dogs for life, and so if one is unsuitable for shows, then there are certainly other ways to get extra enjoyment from a Bernese.

A true evaluation must be made of your Bernese to decide if it is a good representative of the breed. Novice owners may not be the best judges, and even the more experienced owners suffer from biases. But the advice of your dog's breeder will usually bring about an honest, and tactful, opinion. If the breeder of your Bernese is happy for your pride and joy to compete, then everything is set for an introduction to a whole new world. Shows, at varying levels, are organised in many places every week and so your new hobby can be pursued locally or the choice to travel far and wide is available. Advertisements for these shows appear in the weekly dog press, and schedules may also be available at the ringcraft classes which you should try to attend. Other local dog owners may advise where these

A promising show prospect.

Griffiths

show-training classes are held or details of all local clubs are often to be found at the local library, or even via your veterinary surgeon.

Ringcraft classes will provide advice and training for the showring. Both novice owners and seasoned exhibitors use these facilities to socialise and educate young and old dogs in readiness for exhibition. Even if another Bernese owner is not in attendance, valuable knowledge will be gained, not to mention confidence. Puppies can be taken as soon as they are fully vaccinated, and they will soon become accustomed to being handled by strangers. At these classes, an instructor will assume the role of judge, examining each dog thoroughly, indicating a path for the owner to move the dog, and offering advice on how to present the dog to best advantage. Every dog has faults and handling methods suited to minimising weaknesses can be learnt. Not only does your Bernese need to look nice, but he also needs to behave in a calm and steady manner and be happy in the company of other dogs and people. Basic obedience must be employed, and so a very good relationship between dog and handler must be built up: ringcraft classes are just the place to lay these foundations.

Apart from attending these classes, visits to shows should be arranged to watch handling and exhibiting techniques, and to note how Bernese are presented. Different breeds are handled in different ways, although ultimately a suitable method of presenting your dog is the main objective. Experienced exhibitors are able to present their dogs to the judge in a calm and unobtrusive way, and always have their dogs under control and standing in a flattering position. Most Bernese owners are only too happy to share their experience with novices, and useful guidance will be gleaned.

TRAINING FOR A SHOW

Apart from attending classes, much training should be applied at home in readiness for the real thing. A few moments spent every day will soon accustom your Bernese to comply with what is expected and you will be much more confident in knowing that you are both well prepared for the big day. Show dogs are always walked on the left side of the owner and so are moved around the show ring anti-clockwise. At some shows the dogs will be individually examined and moved, but many judges will require the whole class to take part in this initial lap. Your Bernese should move collectedly on a loose lead by your side, being neither too far away from you, nor so close that your movements obstruct the dog from the judge's view. Dogs which pull on the lead will present a very poorly balanced picture, and movement cannot be assessed properly when the dog is dragging the handler along. Choice of lead and collar may help here; it is no good using a fine show lead if more control from a check chain is needed.

Apart from a circuit of the ring, a Bernese will also be required to move straight up and down the ring, in direct line with the judge's line of vision. You will also probably be required to move in a triangular pattern so that rear, side and front movement of your Bernese can be observed, in that order. Movement can be easily practised either in the garden or in parks and open places. Bernese males are often interested in all of the smells on the ground and this should be discouraged, as should the habit of the dog twisting his head to look up at the handler while moving. This will cause the front movement to be impaired, as the natural balance is affected. Lots of praise and encouragement can be employed to get the best from your Bernese, and their natural temperament is such that they love to please, so will learn quickly.

At a show, you will be required to stand your dog so that his outline and stance can be studied, and then a thorough examination by the judge will be made. The judge will look at the overall shape of your Bernese, the way he holds his head and tail, how his legs are placed and how he appears to resemble the ideal dog as set out in the breed standard. For closer examination, the judge will approach the dog from the front and then place his hands on the dog. At this stage, it is vital that your dog is happy to be handled by a stranger and so only those with the correct Bernese temperament should be shown. Any sign of fear or aggression will not only be penalised, but could lead to an unfortunate experience for both the dog and the judge. The judge will look at the overall expression of your Bernese, and then consider the eyes, ear placement, teeth placement and head proportions, before moving along to feel the limbs and body construction. This examination may take a few seconds or may last for a few minutes and the dog is required to stand still throughout. The handler may offer as much praise and verbal assurance as required by the dog, but he should not hinder the judge's inspection.

Once the dog has been handled by the judge, you will be asked to perform the triangular or straight pattern movement, as already mentioned. The judge may then reassess the dog, before you return to the ringside while the next exhibit is considered. In practice, friends and neighbours can be enlisted to go over your Bernese, and of course strangers will be available for practice at classes. Many Bernese will fidget and so in Britain most handlers use a titbit to keep the dog's attention firmly focused on them. In the USA and Canada, Bernese are generally presented on a tight lead, which holds the neck more erect and enables the handler to hold the dog in the required position. In Switzerland, dogs are rarely placed or guided into any position, judges and handlers prefer the dogs to be assessed in a completely natural, if sometimes awkward, stance.

Types Of Show
In Britain there are several types of show. Full details of all types of show, together with complete regulations, are available from the Kennel Club of each country, and I think it is a good idea to obtain a copy of such a publication before you involve yourself in the hobby.

Championship Shows
These are the biggest and most prestigious type of show. Held throughout the country, most breeds will be in attendance, and large breed clubs may also have their own championship each year. Only judges who have received official Kennel Club approval are allowed to officiate, and the highest awards are available. In the UK, challenge certificates are available for the best of each sex, and three CC's must be won from three different judges to qualify for the title of champion, which is every exhibitor's dream. First prizes in certain classes will qualify your Bernese for entry at Cruft's, the most famous and

prestigious dog show in the world. Championship shows are more expensive to enter than smaller shows, but many more dogs are seen in each breed, and so competition is high. These shows are open to all.

OPEN SHOWS

As the name suggests, these events are also open to all, but are not subject to the condition that a bench for each dog must be supplied. Many breeds are scheduled, but there are usually fewer classes for each breed. Even so, the competition is very hot and many exhibitors get great pleasure from confining their activities to this type of show. Inexperienced owners and dogs can also gain extensive experience.

LIMITED SHOWS

These are limited to members of the organising club or society, and only an agreed number of classes, as set by the Kennel Club, can be held. Entry fees are generally very low and some organisers like to give inexperienced judges the opportunity to learn more about judging here.

SANCTION SHOWS

Similar in many ways to Limited Shows, no more than twenty classes can be scheduled. Not very popular in recent years, they can be held as an evening event.

EXEMPTION SHOWS

Exempt from many of the rules governing other shows, these may be lowest on the scale of importance regarding prestige awards, but they are certainly supported and enjoyed by many. Organised as a means of fund-raising for worthy causes, entries are made on the day. Only four classes for pedigree dogs are allowed, with the addition of many fun classes for both pedigree and crossbreeds. Dogs need not be registered at the Kennel Club, and a great variety of mixed breeds will compete in the same classes. As a training ground for inexperienced dogs and handlers, they are unsurpassed. Prizes are usually very generous, with rosettes and other rewards on offer.

MATCHES

Matches are held as a competition between members of clubs or even between two or more clubs. The dogs are judged two at a time on a knockout basis, until only an eventual winner is left. Only a rosette is on offer for the best puppy and the best overall but again a pleasant evening can be enjoyed among friends, while gaining experience along the way.

Once a good basis of understanding has been gathered, then the actual choice of show and entries can be made in preparation for your debut. Advertisements for shows will give an address where a schedule can be obtained. The schedule sets out all the details of the show, a list of the classes, an entry form and other relevant details. It is here that new exhibitors are often confused. Classes are defined by way of age of the dog or by previous wins. Careful choice of the right class is necessary to give your dog the best chance of competing against only those with whom he is comparable. It would be unwise to enter a still underdeveloped sixteen-month-old dog in classes which will be mostly composed of fully mature, not to mention experienced, four- and five-year-olds.

DEFINITIONS OF CLASSES

At championship and open shows, Bernese are usually only entered in one class or possibly two. Special stakes classes are sometimes scheduled, and these may also be supported. In the USA and Canada, one class is commonly the order of the day and in Switzerland dogs are regulated to enter one class only at each show. The entry form must be completed with details of the dog's parentage, date of birth and other details, and entry fees must accompany the entries to arrive by a specified date. Even if you are unable to attend, fees will not be returned.

SHOW PREPARATIONS
Exhibitors

If you are travelling a long way to get to the chosen show, your car must be in perfect order. There are fewer more frustrating experiences then being stranded at the roadside in the early morning after all your plans to get to the show in good time. Subscription to a car recovery service is as essential to those who drive to shows as the dog itself! At one time I used to take a team of between five and eight Bernese to most of the championship shows. The dogs had the comfort of an enormous custom-built trailer which was towed behind the car, and when coupled, the whole thing was longer than a bus. On one occasion, on our way back from a show the car died completely, and when the car mechanic came he could not find the problem so the recovery truck was summoned. If I had not been a member of such an organisation, I do not know how I could have got the dogs home. As it was, the hapless man who came to tow us back could not believe what he saw but at least we reached home safely. Even if you are travelling with only one or two dogs it is worth remembering that dogs are not always happily accepted on public transport and in taxis.

An up-to-date route map should be bought, and of course, this should be taken along on the day. Other local exhibitors will be able to offer a guide for travelling time, as many shows are held at the same venue every year. It is a good idea to make a note of easy routes and also places that the dog can be exercised on the way, for future reference. The car should also be equipped with a first-aid box, water bowl and water container and a non-slip rug or blanket to make sure that your Bernese is comfortable and happy when you arrive at your destination.

If arrangements must be made for those left at home, then be sure to plan well ahead. Your choice of clothing should also be planned for both efficiency and smartness. I see no reason why any owner should go to all the trouble of preparing their exhibit to a high standard and then let the dog down by appearing scruffy. In Britain, many shows are planned for outside, but with limited undercover accommodation, a light but warm waterproof coat and protective footwear should always be taken along. An umbrella can easily be left in the car for emergencies. An exhibitor's attire should be smart without appearing too flamboyant. It is your dog and not you, which needs to catch the judge's attention. Trousers are favoured by many, but a well-cut skirt is also suitable if not too flowing or short. A waist or hip length jacket is less distracting than a long coat which may flap about during movement, and of course, comfortable flat shoes are essential. Heeled shoes have no place at a dog show as exhibitors cannot hope to move the dog smoothly if they are worried about their own balance, and dogs may be injured if inadvertently trodden on. The colour of your clothing should be chosen to complement the colour of the dog. Dark clothing will mask the outline of your dog, so making the judge's job harder, and bold patterns or checks may give a misleading optical illusion. At least one pocket is essential for carrying bait.

A bag containing all the things which are needed at each show can be packed ready to take. Only those things which are necessary should be included, for both your Bernese's comfort and ease of carrying. I would suggest a small, lightweight bowl for water and an empty plastic bottle for water which can be obtained at the show. Some dogs are upset by a change of water caused by the varying mineral and chemical content, and in these cases water from home should be provided. In Britain, all dogs attending a benched show must have a sturdy buckled-type collar and a strong benching chain to attach to the bench. You will also need a show lead and collar, or whatever suits your dog best in the ring. A small towel or absorbent cloth will help dry wet and remove any mud collected at the show, and a comb and brush will be needed for last-minute preparations. A pair of scissors is always useful and a ring-number clip or safety-pin for displaying the number you will receive at the show. In the USA ring-numbers are displayed on armbands, so a few elastic bands could also be added.

Refreshments are usually available at shows, but the queues can be very long which may mean leaving your dog unattended – you may even miss your class. Club shows involve less people than championship or open shows, so the problem is not usually encountered there. A packed lunch can be organised the day before and refrigerated. You will need enough coins to pay for any car park charges, to buy a catalogue and to cover any other expenses. In this way you will avoid the need to wait for change if a note is presented.

Your Bernese

The final preparations for the show involve bathing your Bernese. No matter if his appearance pleases you, he needs a bath to look his best. You can be quite sure that if you don't bath him, you are bound to stand next to another dog at the show who has been properly prepared and your dog will look decidedly grubby. There are very strict regulations laid down regarding the preparation of dogs for exhibition, and so great care must be taken to avoid any products which may leave a residue in the coat.

Full fitness and health come about after many months of correct care and attention, so little can be done at the last minute to change the general condition of your Bernese but a few tips will improve the overall appearance. Bathing should be done ideally two or three days before the show, so enabling the coat to settle down and not appear too fluffy. After bathing, your Bernese should be dried with a hot air drier. If the coat is left to drip dry, it is bound to be flattened and twisted, so giving an uneven look. During drying the coat should be combed in the natural direction of lie, taking out any hairs which have been loosened by the water. Once dry, a little judicious trimming will enhance the dog's appearance, but only a few hairs at a time should be removed as it is very easy to overtrim and the dog will look unsightly.

The hairs on the toes sometimes grow into a point and these can be trimmed to reveal the nice rounded cat-like feet which are so admired. The hair which grows under the pads can also be clipped, but this is a matter for personal choice. The hair which grows as featherings at the back of the front legs should never be trimmed, just combed downwards, as should the hindleg featherings. The hair which grows on the hocks can be quite long on some Bernese, but it should never be trimmed to shorten it. This hair can be combed out at right angles to the leg, and only those hairs which appear out of line should be carefully removed before the hair is combed down to lie along the hock. The site where hind dew claws were located also sends out a few stray hairs which look unsightly, and these too can receive conservative trimming.

The only other areas which may need the attention of your scissors are behind the ears, at the nape of the neck if a small white neck patch is present and at both sides of the chest. I say 'may need' to be trimmed as there is no strict rule about these areas; again it is a matter for choice. Long wisps of hair behind the ears are despised by some owners and greatly admired by others. Judges should not be influenced by such things, but it is a fact that some dogs give the impression of being rather short of neck and stuffy because of the presence of this hair, when in fact the dog is well made and not faulty here. On both sides of the lower chest, hanging down parallel to the front legs, adults have a wisp of long hairs. As your Bernese moves, these hairs will move more than the shorter hairs on the bib, so giving the impression of a rather wavering front action. If just the tips of these hairs are removed to lie in line with the rest of the white bib, an immediate improvement will be seen. Not all Bernese have these, but as a judge I know that many do and they certainly distract your attention when you are studying movement.

A few white hairs on the back of the neck can be removed down to the roots, but their presence will not necessarily mean that the dog will be unduly penalised. If a larger patch is present, then it is best left alone. White hairs will also appear on the body on the site of old injuries, perhaps caused by other dogs in play. These too can be snipped off to advantage, but take care not to be too scissor-oriented. Bernese are a natural breed, and we do not want to fall into the practice of sculpting them with scissors as has happened in many other breeds. This applies particularly to the increasing practice of cutting whiskers. More and more show dogs appear to have these vibrissae removed, as it is thought to give a cleaner appearance to the head and muzzle. There is no good reason to remove these important sensory organs, and any improvement is minimal. They are neither ugly nor distracting to the judge so I see no reason to endorse this practice.

Some owners suggest starving the dog the day before the show, but this is likely to mean that the dog will be without food for some forty-four hours or more until he is fed again after the show. This is cruel, no matter if wild dogs do gorge and starve quite normally.

Domesticated Bernese are used to a feeding routine and a day at the show will disrupt this established routine enough without enforced starvation. I like to feed my dogs at lunchtime the day before a show, so that there is still ample time for the dog to evacuate at home before you set off next day. Bernese are naturally greedy, and so if bait is to be used during exhibition, he will most certainly focus his attention on it without prior starvation.

The bait most frequently used at shows is cooked liver which is cut into small pieces and offered as a reward for attention. Cheese is also regarded as a great delicacy by many dogs and is also sometimes used. But it tends to mess on the handler's fingers, and it sweats when left in a pocket. If liver is to be used, then this must be prepared the day before the show and packed and refrigerated alongside your own packed lunch. There is a valid reason for using liver – it is highly attractive to dogs and only rarely fed so will be eagerly sought as a show day treat.

THE SHOW
When you arrive at the showground, note where the toilets and the dog exercise area are positioned, and look for a tap to fill your water container. The benches at the very large shows are usually stationed near the ring to be used for the judging, but smaller unbenched shows have no real collecting area other than at the ringside.

Once you have found your bearings, put the benching chain and collar on the bench, making sure that it is firmly attached, and then help your Bernese on to the bench to accustom him to it. Never leave a dog unattended on a bench, and at the first few shows make sure that either you or a friend are always at hand to give reassurance. At an unbenched show, lay out the towel from your showbag and settle your dog down near the ringside but well away from the pedestrian path. About fifteen minutes or so before judging is due to begin, take your dog for a walk in the exercise area and then back to the ringside for a final comb-through before you are called for your class.

At the start of each class, a steward will announce the class number and call all those entered to come into the ring. Occasionally ring numbers are attached to the bench at the larger shows, but more often they are given out by the ring steward.

They are worn on the arm in the USA and are clipped on to the chest in Britain. They must be clearly visible and must be worn at all times when in the ring. All the dogs will be stood along the edge of the ring to the left of the judge's table, and the judge will walk along the line of dogs to gain a first impression. Some exhibitors will rush to be one of the first in the line, but novices are better advised to be at least halfway along so that you have plenty of time to watch the procedure, and to give both you and your Bernese time to settle and relax. While you are in the ring, it is a good idea to try to ensure that your dog is either sitting quietly during the judging of the other dogs or standing in a flattering pose. Sometimes judges will glance along the line of waiting dogs, and if your charge is caught with his legs in a poor stance, or showing a dipped topline, the judge may choose to disregard him from the final choice of placed dogs.

When it is your turn to present your dog to the judge, try to remember that you can take your time, as you will have just one chance to show off your dog to his best advantage.

Bernese look more natural when shown on a loose lead. Gaye Sansom's Gillro Ginger Tom.
Hartley

Stand your dog in the same place where the others have stood their dogs, and once settled, stand back slightly so as not to intrude upon the judge's view. If your dog has been trained to stand with a very loose lead, then he is sure to remember his lesson, but if not, try to keep control of your dog by holding the lead taut. Stand on the righthand side of your dog or just in front of him, and try to keep his attention, although refrain from feeding him just before the judge will inspect his mouth. You will not be popular if the judge gets messy liver on his hands, or if he has to wait while the dog finishes chewing and licking his lips.

There are strict rules about not talking to the judge unless you are spoken to, so don't make any comments while he examines your dog. Many judges will ask the age of the dog, and a short and accurate answer is all that is required from you. Some exhibitors will use the dog's name over and over again while the judge is handling the dog in an effort to inform the judge who the dog is, hoping that this may influence placings. Of course, this cheating ploy only works if the dog is called his registered name, and if he has been successful in the show ring before so has some reputation within the breed. There is nothing so offputting to a judge, and sometimes it works against the perpetrator as no judge likes to be considered an easy target for outside influence. If a dog needs verbal control, then it can be done without using a full name for a few moments.

When the examination is over, the judge will direct you where to move the dog. Novices often try to rush, as if they can't wait to get away, but take time to settle your dog. Gather up any looseness of the lead in your left hand, make sure that both you and your Bernese are facing in the same direction and step off smartly at a trot. It can be difficult to walk in a straight line, so fix your gaze on a point and head straight for it. Be sure to note where the judge is standing, and when moving back towards him, aim to stop about six feet away to catch your dog's attention and present him finally front on. The judge may ask you to move again, possibly at an amended speed, but don't get flustered as this does not always indicate that you got it wrong the first time. Likewise, if your dog starts to jump about or pull on the lead and generally disrupt the movement, then stop, compose yourself and scold the dog, and continue on in a more professional manner.

Ordeal over, quickly praise your dog and join the back of the line of waiting dogs while the remainder of the class is assessed. A titbit for good behaviour will be much appreciated by your Bernese, but be sure to keep an eye on the proceedings. Titbits can be an aid to showing, but to an exceptionally greedy dog they can be a hindrance, especially if your dog decides that another exhibitor's bait is decidedly more interesting than your offering! Careful placing can mean that your dog may show himself very well by watching someone else's bait, so capitalise on this situation if you can. If you engage in a short conversation with another exhibitor while waiting, don't be tempted to offer his dog a titbit as a friendly gesture, in case you are later accused of sabotage of the opposition!

With all dogs examined, the steward will sometimes tell exhibitors to again stand their dogs but it really is up to you to take the initiative; so as the judge makes his last evaluation of the dogs you must keep one eye on the judge and the other on your dog, being ready to correct a faulty stance if your dog should move. There are a minority of exhibitors who will use every trick to push their dogs forward, and so if you are crowded without reason or if another dog is placed to obscure you from the judge's view, then be sure to move to present your dog well. Don't be tempted to employ the same tactics, as these cheats are despised by other exhibitors, and such a poor reputation lives with these people for ever.

If you are lucky enough to be asked to bring your dog into the centre of the ring, then it is quite normal to look pleased but there is no reason to go over the top as you have not won until you have the prize card in your hand. Some judges will call out the dogs in the order they will be placed, others will bring out those short-listed, and then reassess them when the rest of the class has been excused from the ring. Most shows offer awards down to fifth place, but some only offer cards to fourth. It is not unknown for the judge to place dogs in order of merit, and then just when you think you have achieved your placing the judge will change his mind and move two or more of the dogs around again. This action is never popular with exhibitors, but it is the judge's prerogative. Keep your dog showing all the time, as when the prize cards are awarded, the judge may want to write a critique on your dog. Conversation between judge and exhibitor is still not allowed unless the judge decides to strike up a question-and-answer session. If you have been first or second in a class, there

Showing can be very rewarding. Ch. Forgeman Footpad. British record holder. Aze

is still a chance that you may be considered for the best of sex or reserve best of sex award. Never be tempted to tell the judge too much about your dog until the breed judging is over. It is always nice to win the first prize in a class, but to be placed is an achievement to be proud of, and you can both be very happy with your award. If you did not win or get placed, then never mind, there is always another day, and another judge. Congratulate the winners in the way that you would like to be congratulated if you had won, and don't be too disheartened or bitter if you were unlucky. There is still the rest of the show to enjoy, and if showing is a hobby that appeals to you, meeting the same people at similar events will mean that you also have new friendships to enjoy.

In Britain, all unbeaten dogs on the day are eligible to compete for the Best of Sex or Best of Breed award at the end of the judging. A Best Puppy award is also sometimes on offer – check the schedule for details. The steward will call winners back into the ring, and the same judging procedure may follow, or the judge may simply look at the dogs in stance, and then give out the results with little delay. A challenge certificate, only on offer at championship shows, is given to the best of each sex. A reserve challenge certificate is also awarded, and this could go to any other class winner or even to the dog placed second in the class won by the CC winner. Eventually the dog CC winner will meet the bitch CC winner for the Best of Breed, and all Best of Breed winners are paraded at the end of the show for the Best of Group awards, and then these finally compete for the Best in Show honour. At open shows, CCs are not on offer, but the final awards are the same and can earn you a good deal of prestige.

In the USA, the title of champion is won by a points system. There are only two types of show, the championship show and the less common sanction show. Points are available at every championship show which schedules the breed, and the number of points depends on the geographical area and the number of dogs entered. The more dogs entered, the more points gained from the best of sex award. To become a champion, three five-point wins (majors) are needed, or a total of fifteen points in all, under at least two different judges. Entries are often much smaller at shows in the USA, and so it is often thought that it is easier to make a dog into a champion there than in Britain. It is a fact that a great number of dogs are made up in the USA every year, whereas very few are in British competitions. The points system may have its failings, but even so each winner has to be the best of those present, and the quality of dogs can be equally high in an entry of twenty as of one hundred and twenty.

In Switzerzerland, the class structure is different, and every dog shown receives a typewritten critique at the time of examination. All the critiques are available for publication, so there is a possibility of public criticism of those judges who make factual errors in judgement. The dogs are not placed in order of merit until each has received a grade, and those with highest grades are in competition to be placed in order of merit to fifth place. Bernese must be at least nine-months-old before they can be shown, and they can only be entered in the Jungendklasse (JK 9-18 months old), dogs and bitches separately. There is also an open class and a champions class, with first to fifth placings in these. To be awarded the title of champion, three CACs, which is the top award for the best of each sex, must be won under three different judges who are breed specialists at regional or club shows. The title of international champion is gained by winning four CACIBs, which are only on offer to the best of each sex at international shows. At least one year must elapse from the winning of the first and qualifying award. The most noticeable difference in the whole judging process is that there is no hurry to process a production line of dogs quickly. And much more stamina is needed by both dogs and handlers as countless laps of the ring may be required to assess movement.

CHAPTER ELEVEN

Breeding

In a world which is grossly overpopulated with dogs – pedigree and cross-bred, wanted and unwanted – your motives for wanting to add to the Bernese population should be examined. Breeding Bernese is a very enjoyable hobby, but it is not without its problems, and heartache is often experienced by enthusiasts. Owners need not have intelligence or experience to breed dogs; the dogs manage very well without our interference in most cases. But whether you plan to breed one litter or a number of litters over the next few years, the responsibilities are the same. I have often heard people say: 'I'm not a real breeder, I just wanted to have some puppies from my bitch.' Real breeder or not, whatever that may mean, the task should not be undertaken lightly.

Across the world, many dog-lovers are attracted to the Bernese for his undoubted qualities. Breeding from a Bernese bitch may only appeal after a period of ownership, or it may occur where a breeding prospect is consciously sought. Either way, it is a long-term project: the puppies from a single litter remain a responsibility for the breeder long after they have been sold into new homes and ownership. Breed rescue organisations may well exist, but that should make no difference to the breeders' true responsibility of looking after everything they have decided to bring into the world. Even if you own the most wonderful specimen of the breed and are keen to embark on a project of breeding, you will not be able to do so for the benefit of the breed or your own dogs, unless you have the time, facilities and resources. Too many novice breeders panic when puppies remain unsold after the usual time for them to join new families; the feeding costs and extra work involved in caring for and training these growing youngsters can be a burden.

Pedigree dog breeding, involving a large breed such as the Bernese, is not a paying hobby on a small scale. Certainly, there will be an income of cash when puppies are sold, but this has usually been spent, plus more, in keeping your bitch and paying vet fees, as well as the costs involved with the actual litter. Income received from the sale of puppies will offset some of your costs, but it is immoral to breed puppies for sale purely to finance your own dogs. You need enough money to rear a litter until it is four or five months old, if necessary, and to pay for a caesarean operation or any treatment needed during a difficult whelping, and for any advertising, before you proceed any further with your breeding plans. The facilities needed for rearing a litter are a matter of opinion. Some breeders will want to rear the puppies in a kennel with access to an outside run or pen; others will want to have the puppies in the house, for a time at least. Puppies need space to run and play, and if kept in an area which is too small, they will become bored and soiled.

I have kept the subject of time until the last, but in fact it is one of the most important aspects of breeding. Adult Bernese need a lot of attention from their owners, and puppies' needs are tenfold in this respect. Newly born puppies need to be watched carefully when with their mother, to prevent accidents. When they are weaned, they will need to be taught how to eat and to be washed afterwards! As they become more aware of their surroundings, puppies need human contact to develop the natural Bernese temperament. As they grow older, puppies need to be taught how to behave in the house and out-of-doors, and socialisation cannot be hurried nor taught too well.

If you have the happy situation whereby you are confident that a litter of Bernese could be accommodated within your home, then you must embark upon a course of educating yourself further about the breed. It is not enough to be keen and willing to learn. The knowledge you have now is worth twice that which you may acquire in future. I do feel that an apprenticeship within the breed should be served before going ahead to breed. We all hope that we will enrich the breed with the puppies we decide to bring into the world, but reality often disappoints us. Even the best laid plans can bring about an unexpected result, but you cannot expect a good result without knowledge and planning. People can always cite a case when a very mediocre bitch was mated to a reasonable dog and a wonderful Bernese was the result. This does happen, but is little help to the breed; and for a long-term project, you will soon learn that one-off Bernese never make good foundation stock for the future. The tired old tale that 'we are breeding for the improvement of the breed' is oft repeated but rarely meant. True knowledge is needed to help the breed progress and that means knowledge not only about individual dogs but also about bloodlines and compatible families. We all had to start somewhere and much is learned from experience; but a good foundation in Bernese matters is as necessary as learning the Highway Code before taking a driving test.

ASSESSING BREEDING POTENTIAL

Owners who are keen to breed and who own a bitch must ask themselves several questions and answer them truthfully. No matter how often one is tempted to be economical with the truth to others, nothing will be gained by trying to fool yourself.

1. Does your bitch come from bloodlines which have sound, healthy, typical Bernese in great depth?
2. Is she good enough to breed – with particular emphasis on temperament, soundness and type?
3. No Bernese is perfect, but does she have faults in greater numbers than attributes?
4. Does your skill as a breeder, and her breed qualities, make her an asset for the breed as far as you can predict?

More and more Bernese puppies are bred every year, some good and some not so good. It is obviously more difficult to place puppies when there are lots of litters looking for good homes, so what can your Bernese offer the breed that is not already on offer from a more experienced, established breeder? None of us can claim to have been an expert at the start.

Ch. Jumbo v Waldacker at Coliburn and Rena v Lyssbach at Coliburn showing a similarity of type necessary for breeding consistency, pictured with Jude Simonds.

I have bred some forty litters. I am still learning – and I am sure that the majority of realistic breeders would say the same. No matter how much you love your Bernese as a companion, it might not be good enough to breed from. If faults appear which are unacceptable – then those producers should be withdrawn from the gene pool.

The Brood Bitch

1. *Her pedigree and ancestors:* Before looking at any individual, it is important to know what faults and virtues are to be found in as many of her relatives as can be seen and researched. Some faults, especially those which affect the wellbeing of the individual Bernese, are more serious than those which are cosmetic. But any fault which recurs is to be avoided in future breeeding. Some faults are widespread throughout the breed, and if these same faults appear in a great number of your bitch's ancestors, then there are two points for further consideration.

 i. If the condition is so widespread, why should you worry about it since most breeders are in the same position?

ii. Is it feasible to try to find a bitch who is not likely to be carrying the same fault?

   Your answers to these questions will indicate whether you are a breeder who can be respected or someone who just wants to breed pretty Bernese puppies. Bernese are a wonderful breed, but there is certainly room for improvement in both type and

Franzi v Gitzirain, 8½ weeks in whelp.   Schlucter

soundness. Every breeder should have this in mind and be aiming high with each planned mating.

In the UK, there is a high incidence of foreleg lameness within the breed. A survey carried out a few years ago highlighted some worrying patterns, and the geneticists' report indicated that the problem could be inherited to some degree. Owners with dogs suffering from this weakness can be given advice but it is little comfort for them to be told that the puppy's father and grandfather had the same problem. Even if both improved after treatment, this is not the way to help the breed progress. Veterinary science and surgical techniques have improved tremendously over recent years, and it is quite right that any dog should benefit from new developments to reduce suffering. But these new advances should not allow breeders to be complacent. It is not enough to simply correct defects – they should be bred out.

2. *Your bitch's individual qualities*: The most important characteristic of a Bernese is a good temperament: that means biddable, intelligent, calm and steady. Excuses are often made: 'She was dropped as a puppy', 'she was once frightened by a man', and any number of other reasons as to why the bitch behaves as she does. Behaviour can be influenced by events and feeding, but for the most part puppies will learn from their dam's reactions, and whether her characteristics are hereditary or not, she will pass on her attitudes to her puppies. If she is very excitable or apprehensive, the puppies are likely to be the same.

So a brood bitch should have a perfect temperament above all else. She should be absolutely sound and should have a history of good health and fitness. Any bitch which has received surgery to correct osteochondritis dissecans or entropion or any other debilitating defect should never be considered for breeding. The hip status of your bitch may affect your final decision, but there are no set rules as to what is acceptable or not on an individual level. On the Continent there are rules regarding what hip grades are allowed for breeding, but in the UK and the USA it is up to the individual to decide. The breed average is published in many countries and ideally your bitch should fall into this category.

The ideal brood bitch should be broad and sturdy, although feminine. She should also be within the breed standard for height – although many small bitches are bred from – and she should have substance. Her head should be broad and kind, with correct eyes and teeth placement. Her markings should be classic – middle of the road with no exaggerations. In the past there has been a tendency for over-marked Bernese to do well in the show ring and consequently to be used for breeding. This has brought about an increase in over-marked puppies. The markings are important but it must be remembered that this is only one aspect of the breed. If I had the choice of an under-marked or an over-marked bitch, who were the same in every other respect, I would choose the under-marked every time, as she will breed correct markings more easily. The original Swiss standard called for slight-to-medium white blaze, and too much white on legs and neck and around the anus was mentioned as an undesirable fault. Breeders should concentrate on this and discard personal preferences. No bitch is perfect. Any bitch is bound to have her faults; but she should have that definite look of quality . . . anything less, and she should lead a happy life as your companion only. Breeders can justify using any and every Bernese for breeding, but the breed deserves only the very best, even if that means personal disappointment.

If you have decided that it would be wise to purchase a well-bred puppy with the intention to breed in the future, then even more time must be taken to choose a puppy with the best potential than when buying a puppy as a companion. You will gain experience by owning your first Bernese, and this can be put to good use. Visit as many shows as you can, not just to log the winners but to look at the individual dogs and note those that are of the type you admire. Some prolific breeders will have a large number of dogs in the show ring, while other stock appears more rarely. This should have no bearing on your final decision, as it is the quality of foundation Bernese which is of prime importance. Buying from the most successful show kennel may be a ticket to instant success; But it may also prove a hindrance when selling puppies, as you will have similar stock to many others. Personally, I have always thought that it is vital for the breed to have a number of breeding colonies from different genetic backgrounds. If an undesirable genetic defect appears, as in the case of Hypomyelinogenesis in the UK, there still are a number of quality dogs from which to breed, and the affected lines can be avoided, if desired. Having said that, there is nothing to be gained from being different just to make a point. The over-riding principle to bear in mind is that only Bernese of excellence should be bred from.

Once a suitable breeder has been located, with the typical, healthy Bernese that you so wish to start breeding with, then patience will probably be needed. Your ideal puppy may not appear for some months, but it is important to wait for the right puppy, and not just take any one that comes along from your chosen bloodlines. The breed will not deteriorate if your breeding activities are slightly delayed. Be sure to state your hopes and plans for the future when booking a puppy. Then, if you have done your homework and research thoroughly, pray for luck and good fortune, because you still have a long way to go.

THE STUD DOG

Many owners of male Bernese may be attracted to the idea of breeding, but without the hassle of rearing and selling puppies. It is commonly thought that a sexually aware dog will be an excellent candidate for stud use. How wrong this can be! A sex maniac is no good to anyone, and the dog will most likely become unhappy in the long term. If you do want to become involved with the breeding scene, then you must consider the following questions:

1. Will you take responsibility for the offspring from your dog if the breeder is unable to? Could you help with rehousing or could you look after another dog temporarily when you already have a male in the house?

2. Are you prepared to risk a change in attitude from your Bernese if he becomes too assertive or hyperactive because you used him at stud for reasons which were of more benefit to you than him?

3. Are you experienced enough to know if your Bernese has something to offer the breed for its development, or is your dog similar to many others?

4. Are you under the impression that you will become influential within the circle of breed enthusiasts? Or do you think that owning a stud dog is an easy way to make a healthy income?

In an ideal world, the breeder of puppies should take responsibility for ensuring that these Bernese have a happy and settled future. However, sometimes breeders cannot or will not see to the wellbeing of dogs which cannot stay with their original owners. Surely the owner of the sire of the litter is second in line for this responsibility? If you could not offer help by taking an unwanted Bernese in, would you be prepared to help with rehabilitation costs? Most Bernese males, if carefully reared, are well adjusted and delightful companions. The risk that his temperament may be altered by stud use warrants careful consideration. Introduction to sexual activity could change his attitude to everyday happenings drastically. I am sure that there will be some people who do not understand why I say this. It is true that some dogs experience no change in temperament at all, remaining the same calm and placid pets they always were. But these dogs are usually owned by sensible people, who have a very real relationship of trust and respect before introducing their dog to stud activities. Once a change in attitude occurs, the damage is done and may be irreparable. Relaxed dogs can become constantly aware, perhaps leading to hyperactivity. The normally obedient dog may find that his new-found instincts are much stronger than his responses to his owner's commands. Scent marking can become a major pastime – in your house as well as during walks. Loss of condition can occur due to frustration caused by a lack of visiting bitches for service. Even the scent of local bitches in season will cause more fretful anxiety than before the dog was used as a sire. Misplaced sexual attention to people can also occur, most frequently directed towards children and menstruating women. Sexual attention to other male dogs may also be exhibited, and resentment can cause fights between dogs. Few dogs are used at stud frequently, unless they are of outstanding merit. Such a male is likely to be satisfied sexually and so is less likely to exhibit problem behaviour. But it is possible that the first bitch may be the last, and if he becomes sexually frustrated, then you as the owner will have to cope.

Stud fees may seem a welcome bonus to the household income, but there are also outgoings. A dog used at stud must be fed the very highest quality feedstuffs and he must be kept in the peak of condition. If he is to be used regularly, then periodic veterinary checks must be made to ensure that he is free from infection which may be passed on to visiting bitches or which might affect his fertility. To maintain his status you may need to take him to shows more often than you would like. Family plans may have to be changed to accommodate owners of visiting bitches, as the correct day for a bitch to be mated cannot be accurately predicted. Entertaining the accompanying family, all eager to watch the proceedings, may be a time-consuming and costly process, especially if the mating doesn't happen too quickly.

You may feel that I have not been too encouraging to novice owners who want their dogs to be used at stud. Correct! I have seen several owners left with a very different Bernese after he has experienced the joys of bitches. Apart from breed qualities, a very special kind of temperament is needed in a stud dog, and without that I feel that the gamble is not worth taking.

CHOOSING A MATE

Most novice owners of Bernese would be wise to contact the breeder of their bitch for advice regarding the choice of suitable bloodlines and of individual Bernese. An in-depth knowledge of pedigrees is more important than using a top winner because he is in demand – what may suit one bitch may not be right for another. If the breeder of your bitch has experience gained over a number of years, then the best advice is bound to come from that direction. Some stud dog owners will be happy to suggest that their male is the ideal choice, and they may be absolutely correct. Listen to all the advice that is given, but the final decision is yours. You will be responsible for the puppies and answerable to their future owners, so you must be completely happy with your final choice of mate.

GENETICS AND BREEDING PRACTICES

Genes are the unique individual characteristics which are carried in body cells, and will determine, to a very great extent, how a dog will look and behave, although outside influences can also come into play. Genes are carried within the body on chromosomes and dogs have thirty-nine pairs of these. Each pair consists of one chromosome from the dam and one from the sire. Genes come together in a completely random selection in the fertilized embryos, which will explain why there is great variation between some littermates and between different litters from the same parents. Certain features of the Bernese involve several genes, and genes are not all equal. Dominant genes are those points which show up on an individual dog, and recessive genes are those which remain unseen until they combine with a similar gene at a mating and so become apparent in one or more offspring.

The only way to know what genes are carried by your bitch and a prospective stud dog is by researching into the characteristics of siblings, close relatives and any offspring already produced. A dog with a gay tail may always produce gay tails, but he may also produce a large number of correct tails. Two parents are needed for each puppy, and so knowledge about both is needed before any real conclusions can be drawn. Many of the faults seen in Bernese are thought to be produced by recessive genes: cleft palates, incorrect teeth placement, hypomyelinogenesis, to name but three. With the latter condition, some stud dogs have sired many litters before an affected puppy has been produced, and although a few owners still argue for the genetic inheritance of the condition, all the litters containing unaffected puppies would indicate that the dams may not have been carrying a similar gene. However, both the dominant and recessive genes are passed on to offspring, and so will continue in this stock.

There are many books on genetics which go into great detail for dog breeders. Genetics is not new – genes have always been involved with the breeding of any animal; but it is only recently that breeders have been encouraged to take a more scientific interest. Whether you decide to learn from books or not, you should certainly learn from observing your results: details of all dogs used for breeding and of each of the puppies produced should be carefully collected for future reference.

The three most common breeding practices are line-breeding, in-breeding and out-crossing. There are a number of conflicting views on the benefit of each, and explanations from different breeders may vary. But one fact is relevant to all breeding practices: only those characteristics which are present in the genes can be reproduced. Problems which are definitely inherited, such as an undershot or overshot mouth, can only appear if they are carried within the genes of the dogs which appear in the pedigrees of either or both parents. No breeding practice can be credited with powers which do not already lie within.

Line-breeding and in-breeding both involve mating animals which are related. Line-breeding usually refers to joining together two pedigrees which carry related stock of excellence in an effort to concentrate the qualities of one or two outstanding relatives. When breeding for a particular type, line breeding can help intensify the desired traits more quickly than mating together unrelated dogs. But the undesired traits will also be intensified, so great care must be taken to line-breed to outstanding Bernese and not just for the sake of following a trend. Many established colonies of Bernese and other breeds are recognisable by the consistent appearance of the dogs produced, and in most cases these dogs will be line-bred. The most common form of line-breeding is to mate a successful sire to one of his granddaughters or perhaps mate together Bernese with several common ancestors three or four generations back in the pedigree. Line-breeding is in fact a less intense method of in-breeding, but is perhaps a safer way to breed even if slower than in-breeding for fixing points.

In-breeding is the mating together of very close relatives – mother to son, father to daughter or even half or full brother and sister. The genes will be intensified, and in the hands of an experienced breeder, knowledge can be gained quickly about what traits are carried by any particular bloodline. Any kind of breeding is experimental; you can never completely predict the end result from even the best laid plans. If poor results appear, a particular bloodline can be abandoned, but there is still the placement of puppies to consider. In-breeding on outstanding Bernese is likely to bring about good results, but will also highlight the problems. Continual in-breeding is thought to reduce fertility and hybrid vigour, and so unrelated Bernese will need to be incorporated at intervals to counteract and, hopefully, to improve defects as they are recognised. In some breeds in-breeding is common, but in Bernese it is seldom practised.

Out-crossing is the mating together of animals which are completely unrelated, at least for the first four generations. If you trace pedigrees back far enough there will usually be common ancestors, but it is generally thought that the first three generations have the most influence on offspring. Complete out-crossing is sometimes practised for each generation, but within a limited gene pool this will prove difficult. Both line-breeding and in-breeding may involve out-crossing from time to time, but then the resulting dogs are bred back into the line. If a novice owner desperately wants to breed from a Bernese bitch who can only claim reasonable type and has an undistinguished family, then the sole hope for improving future generations is to out-cross to a Bernese from a proven quality background. Then each resultant litter must be carefully assessed to decide which breeding practice should be followed for continued success.

Whatever breeding practice is followed, a constant assessment of stock is essential for progress. Breeders must always remember it is not necessary to breed from every Bernese; those that are simply not good enough still have a place as companions. It is equally important to realise that there is no such thing as a perfect Bernese. There is no point in placing undue importance on minor faults as long as overall progress is clearly made with each generation. It would be a very clever and fortunate breeder who could improve every aspect of a Bernese in one generation.

Breeding for Type

Type is often spoken of, but seldom understood. Type is not easy to define, but is recognisable to breed enthusiasts who have taken the time to learn about and observe the breed thoroughly. Type is perhaps best explained as the characteristics which separate Bernese from any other large, similarly marked breed. It is the very essence of a true Bernese Mountain Dog.

Type is essential in every Bernese, as without it you do not have a real Bernese. It is possible to have a Bernese with several faults, but for it still be of excellent type, and it is also possible to have a Bernese without any outstanding fault but is distinctly lacking in type. One person's idea of type may differ quite considerably from another's, but type is easily recognisable in some bloodlines. A visit to a show or to a breeder may give the opportunity of seeing a number of related Bernese which may be similar: they may not all be of true type but they will show a family type. It is this family likeness that makes dogs from one particular kennel easily recognisable, and owners of such Bernese have not established these similarities by chance.

The only way to establish a type is to mate Bernese of similar characteristics for several generations. Line-breeding can bring this about quickly, but out-crossing will achieve the same result if a mating takes place between two similar Bernese. If each unrelated family is itself line-bred, then less variation in the resultant puppies will be seen. Breeding for a particular type is a most satisfying, but difficult, process. The goal of all breeders is to produce litter after litter with the same family likeness, establishing a recognisable and admired type.

THE ONSET OF THE SEASON

If your Bernese bitch is to be mated on or after her third season, then the oestrus cycle can be predicted with some accuracy. Some bitches will come into season at exact six monthly periods; others have nine months or even a year between seasons. It is not unknown in the breed for bitches to come into season with only three or four months between each bleeding, and the wisdom of breeding from these is questionable. The ability to reproduce normally is inherited the same way as many other characteristics, and to introduce such a weakness into the breeding programme could be most unwise for future generations.

About a month before your bitch is due to come into season when you plan to breed from her, she should be wormed and her vaccinations should be brought up to date, if necessary. Her general condition should be excellent and she should be near the peak of her fitness. I recommend that a multi-vitamin supplement should be added to her food if there is any chance that her diet may be lacking in any way. The addition of a wheatgerm and vitamin E capsule each day is thought to help fertility. Any minor complaints such as skin or ear problems should be treated, so that she is absolutely well and without risk of infection.

The first sign that your bitch is about to come into season may be an increase in the number of times she urinates. She may leave small amounts of urine at regular intervals in an effort to scent-mark her own territory and when out for exercise. There may also be a slight enlargement of the vulva – her external genital organ – and if other dogs are kept, she may begin to attract attention. The season proper begins when a blood-stained discharge is seen. Most commonly owners notice smears on the floor, but if the bitch is to be mated then I would suggest that she is examined both morning and night to be sure that the very first signs of the coloured discharge are recognised. Novice owners may find it useful to test for colour by gently pressing a small piece of white tissue on to the vulva, as even the creamy-coloured discharge which sometimes precedes the blood can be easily seen in this way. The first blood-stained discharge will be a bright red, and rather watery; only as the season progresses will the colour darken, until somewhere between the eighth and fourteenth day the discharge will change yet again.

As soon as the first signs of a blood-stained discharge are seen, the owner of the sire you have chosen as the prospective mate should be contacted immediately. Although the exact day of mating cannot be predicted, at least you can give some idea so that there will be minimum disruption to plans. Some stud owners will insist that any bitch presented for mating must have a vaginal smear test to ensure that no infection is present which could be passed on. Your own vet will advise on this, but generally you will need to take the bitch to the vet as soon as possible so that a smear can be taken, and then a culture will be grown to see what is present. It is normal for some bacteria to be present in the vaginal tract, but other infections will render the bitch incapable of conception and possibly cause sterility if passed on to the stud.

From the onset of the season, the bitch should not be left unattended if there is any possibility of a dog gaining access to her. Even inexperienced bitches can find themselves mated by a wily male so vigilance is needed at all times. It is probably wise not to exercise her near the house. If you wish to avoid the neighbourhood strays making a nuisance of themselves, take the bitch some distance by car before exercising her. Not only is it possible for a dog to gain access to your garden and mate the bitch, but there could be complaints from neighbours if your bitch's scent has attracted strays who will themselves cause noise and mess. Do not be tempted to use any form of deodorant spray to mask the smell of her sexual attraction. Most males with an ounce of intelligence will not be fooled, but inexperienced stud dogs may well be put off by the odour and even bathing a bitch may not remove all traces.

A bitch can only conceive if she is ovulating at the time of the mating. I have known some bitches to lose a deep blood red-stained discharge throughout their season. But in most, the colour of the discharge will change, so giving a good idea of when the optimum time for service will be. The vulva will become very enlarged, and this is easily noticeable if she has been inspected every day, and the discharge will change into a very pale pink colour or even be completely colourless. This will herald the correct time for mating, and a call to the stud dog owner to arrange a visit at a mutually convenient time should be made. In an experienced bitch – one who has been mated before – the behaviour patterns may also change up to and during ovulation. Bitches kept together will often display sexual awareness and will mount one another and pay a lot of attention to each other's sexual organs. During grooming sessions, a bitch may push her rear end towards you and even turn her tail to one side if her lower back or thighs are tickled or scratched. Maiden bitches may not exhibit any of these signs, and the individual temperament of bitches will affect their behaviour.

In their enthusiasm to get the bitch mated, many owners take the bitch to the stud for service before she is ovulating, resulting in failure to conceive. The fact that a bitch or dog shows a keenness to mate does not indicate fertility. From my experience, I would suggest that owners take their Bernese bitch to the stud dog at least 24 hours after the discharge turns very pale or colourless. It is true that some bitches ovulate for longer than others, but if there are few eggs released then the sperm will have less chance of successful fertilisation. An ovulation test is on offer from most veterinary surgeons. This, however, cannot predict the condition, it can only tell when the bitch is or is not ovulating. But this test may be very useful to an owner who has to travel a very long distance to visit the stud, so it is worth consideration. At this point, I feel it prudent to mention that it is a little unfair to use your own male as a tester of the readiness-for-mating a bitch, if she is to be presented elsewhere for mating. You should never tease any male like this; it can cause only frustration and resentment.

Most books state that the majority of bitches will be ready for mating between the tenth and fourteenth day after the onset of the season. This may be so, but each bitch is different and each may vary from season to season. I have had bitches conceive from matings as early as eight days and as late as the eighteenth day. Each bitch is a law unto herself, so a careful watch on her behaviour and obvious signs of discharge change should help decide. Often novice owners will try to fit the mating in with their plans; and it can be more convenient to arrange a time at weekends. I can clearly remember one man, whose bitch had failed to conceive at the first mating. He then presented his bitch on a Thursday afternoon during two successive seasons as it was his half day! Sometimes the timing of a mating will work out ideally, but often it will mean some disruption to normal activities, so owners really must get their priorities right. The stud dog owner cannot be expected to change work schedules to accommodate you, so it is not unfair for them to suggest a mating at their convenience on your chosen day. Although a fee will be paid to the owner of the stud dog, you will have to make the sacrifices to fit around the stud dog owner's plans. This will, in fact, be one of many inconveniences you will have to bear if you intend to breed Bernese.

Some owners may be offered the facility of leaving a bitch with the stud owner for a few days, if there are going to be insurmountable travelling problems or some other difficulty. There are pros and cons about this. Leaving a bitch with the stud owner will mean that she can be mated over several days if necessary, so increasing the chance of a fertile mating. But she may be unduly stressed at the separation from her owner, which is not conducive to a successful outcome. Most stud owners will not have the facilities for an in-season bitch to stay, and the disruption of such an interesting visitor may not be welcome to all. Think very carefully before deciding. If the option seems viable, you should be confident that your bitch has the temperament which enables her to adapt to new people and that she has a few days to settle in and get used to her environment before she is ready for mating. Most maiden bitches will be a little upset at being of such interest to a male, and the presence and encouragement of her owner will help her understand that all is well.

THE MATING

Once the owner of your chosen stud dog has been told of your imminent visit, he should refuse any other bitch for service by the same dog for three days before and three days after your expected service. Although a healthy male is capable of mating several bitches over a short period of time, it is courtesy to give your bitch exclusive use of the male, and the risk of passing infection from one bitch to another will be lessened. You may have been asked to have your bitch swab-tested to prove her health status, so it is only fair to expect the same healthy state in the male.

I think that it is better not to feed either the dog or the bitch on the day of the mating, prior to the service. A light meal could be offered in the morning if an evening mating has been organised, but is really not necessary. Likewise, it would be unwise to take the male on a marathon exercise jaunt just before he is expected to perform. Both dog and bitch should have had ample time and opportunity to relieve themselves prior to introduction, and it will be much appreciated by the stud dog owner if the bitch has emptied herself before arrival at the male's premises.

Prompt arrival is a matter of courtesy, as the family and other dogs on the premises may have to be accommodated elsewhere during your visit. If the weather is very hot, then a shaded area is essential, or failing that, a place inside, out of the heat and sunshine. Wet weather is usually tolerated more easily by the dogs than by their owners, but again a place in shelter would be a good idea. An inconspicuous observer should not cause any problems. Two experienced handlers are ideal to oversee or help with the mating of two large dogs, but a third person can be useful at times.

In the chosen area, the two Bernese should be allowed a few moments to look at each other before proceeding any further. A bitch can be rather upset by the over amorous attentions of some males, and a few moments spent allowing her to become accustomed to the idea of the male, is usually time well spent. The owner of the stud will usually take charge of the proceedings and if he is experienced he will know what is best to bring the mating about. Some bitches will behave in an almost shameless fashion to entice the dog to mate them, others can be rather afraid of the unusual circumstances. It is not unknown for some Bernese bitches to be rather too humanised and not react instinctively to the advances of the male, even at the most receptive time of their season. I find that in these cases, it is best to be kind but firm with the bitch in order to get the mating over as soon as possible and cause her the minimum of stress.

If your bitch should resist the advances of the stud dog, this does not mean that she is unready. In an ideal world everything would happen naturally; not so with domesticated species. If the two Bernese do not form an immediate union, then a little human help will make the pairing less traumatic for all concerned. Some bitches may show aggression to the male and owners can be horrified at this side of the character which may not have been witnessed before. Most often this is the reaction of uncertainty and not real viciousness. Do not worry if the stud owner wants to muzzle the bitch's mouth: it is for protection of the stud dog, the handler of the bitch and the bitch herself. Accidents can happen in a moment of confusion, so it is best to be safe. Even those bitches which object violently will settle down as soon as they are tied to the dog and so any restraint can then be removed from them.

A reluctant bitch can be forced, if necessary, to accept the male, but a reluctant male cannot be induced to mate a bitch unless he is interested to some degree. It is vital not to upset the male during a mating and his safety must be guarded, although some dogs become keener if the bitch shows vocal resistance. And inexperienced male could be put off forever if he is mishandled. If the bitch is willing to be mated, then she could be mated within a matter of minutes if you are lucky. Experience on the part of the stud handler will tell if a bit more time will help to achieve a mating without human interference, but the comfort of both the Bernese must be the most important factor. Some bitches will misbehave in the presence of their owners and may be unnerved by an anxious atmosphere. Some owners are best kept away and then brought back to comfort their bitch during the tie. Of course, if the distress caused upsets the owner, then there is no need to pursue the mating at all.

In some cases, the bitch will need to be held firmly by her collar, while another attendant kneels down at her right side and holds her tail to the side. The dog will then mount the bitch, after licking and inspecting her vulva. He will wrap his front legs around her waist and clasp her tightly. As soon as his penis has penetrated her vagina, his thrusting movements will become frantic but after a time he will seem more settled and steady. At this point, he may turn himself, or need help to drop both front legs down on the same side of the bitch and then lift his hind leg over her back so that the pair are turned back-to-back. Both dog and bitch should be held at the collar to prevent them moving about or pulling away from each other and this is best achieved by manoeuvring them against a fence or wall. I like to arrange their tails so that they are not both at the same side, as this seems to help the pair to be more comfortable.

The ejaculation of the male occurs in three parts. The first fluid passed is thought to be a mixture of semen and any other residue which was in the penis, and this is passed within a second or two. The sperm is passed within one or two minutes of penetration while the dog is still on top of the bitch thrusting determinedly. Each drop of semen contains many thousands of sperm, and these are helped on their way up into the bitch by the seminal fluid which follows as a drip feed during the rest of the tie period. A tie is always preferable in a mating, but bitches can and do conceive by a slip mating as long as the male organ is held inside the bitch for a few minutes. The tie is caused by the swollen bulb, the bulbus glandis, at the base of the penis which is held by the muscles of the bitch's vagina. The tie can last for just a few minutes or much longer, usually around twenty to thirty minutes. When the swollen bulb decreases in size, then the two dogs will part and the mating is over. At the moment of separation, some of the seminal or prostatic fluid may be expelled by the bitch. This is nothing to worry about: the majority of the ejaculate will have travelled far enough up into the bitch for fertilisation to take place. The male should then be removed to a quiet place without the interference of other dogs so that he may clean himself. The bitch should not be allowed to run about, as most frequently bitches are extremely pleased with themselves and behave quite skittishly.

I prefer not to let my bitches pass water for at least half an hour after a mating, although I don't suppose that too much semen should be washed away if a tie has taken place. Visiting bitches should be put into the car to settle after the experience. I believe that stress may have a major influence on whether a bitch conceives or not, and so any upset caused during the mating should be quickly forgotten.

ONE MATING OR TWO?

For any bitch to conceive, it is, of course necessary for the mating to take place while she is ovulating. Only a very few of the sperm are needed to fertilise her eggs and the semen will live for some time within the bitch before the excess dies. As long as a mating takes place during ovulation, then one mating should suffice, although two matings spaced thirty-six to forty-eight hours apart are advised to be sure and to give reassurance to the owner. The breeding contract with the stud dog owner should clarify the position.

Once the mating is complete, do not impose on the time of the stud dog owner as they are invariably busy people. Do not always expect a guided tour of the premises, as not only will you have the scent of your bitch which may upset other dogs, but there is also a risk of infection from a visiting dog, especially if there are puppies on the premises. The stud fee should be paid at the time of mating, and the signed stud receipt and registration form for the resulting litter should also be signed and handed to you. If the bitch should fail to conceive, find out if a free service is offered to the same bitch next season. Most stud owners offer this service, but not all. The stud fee you have paid is for the actual mating, not the guaranteed birth of a litter. It bears repeating here, that there is a responsibility to keep breeders informed of the progress and wellbeing of the puppies. If any undesirable traits manifest themselves in the progeny, the breeder can consider the wisdom of breeding further stock from the same parents.

CHAPTER TWELVE

Whelping

PREGNANCY in a normal healthy Bernese bitch is something which she will endure without fuss or bother. Usually it is the inexperienced owner who feels that more should be done during this time. Once a bitch has been mated, then there is very little to do. I like to feed a multi-vitamin supplement from the start of the season if the bitch is being fed a mixed diet. Those bitches fed on a complete food will need no extras at all. However, even though the quantity of food offered need not be increased for a few weeks, the quality of the food should be the highest. There will soon be great demands upon the bitch, so it is vital that she is functioning efficiently.

For the first month, it is perhaps best to try to forget about the possibility of pregnancy in your Bernese and just go about your usual routine. Exercise should not be decreased because of her delicate condition; she should be kept fit and well which will aid a natural whelping when the time comes. She should not be allowed to become fat or lazy; this may contribute to problems later. Bernese bitches may prove difficult to confirm as being in whelp, as I have found that after mating most just seem to think pregnant. Even if conception has not taken place, Bernese bitches are very maternal and can easily convince themselves and those around them that they are carrying puppies. No two bitches are exactly alike, but many will show behavioural signs which you as the owner may interpret as encouraging. Some bitches will start to take great care of themselves and will not be keen to run about as much as is usual. They may also seek more human company, or the opposite, seek seclusion. Nearly all will become more loving and demand your attentions.

The first physical signs will be a bloom on the coat; she will look very well indeed. The vulva will not quite return to the normal size, remaining slightly enlarged and fleshy, although there is no sign of discharge. The teats will be rather reddened, those nearer the rear being more obviously flushed than those near the ribcage. The redness is due to the increased blood supply, and they will become rather erect and hardened during the first four weeks. Morning sickness may occur about three weeks after mating, when a frothy yellow bile is expelled. This is no cause for worry, as the appetite is not usually impaired by this sickness.

During the first week following fertilisation, the ovum is dividing into a mass of cells and begins to make its way toward the uterus. The tiny embryos do not begin to attach themselves to the horns of the uterus until about the twentieth day. At about half-an-inch in size, they are too small to detect by manipulation. From the third to the fourth week, all the organs of the body are forming, and the embryo will begin to curl up into the classic recognisable foetus position. By the end of the fourth week, the individual foetus will be about two inches long. From about four and a half weeks, the sexual characteristics are developing in the individuals.

As the development of the foetuses is rapid, any event which causes stress to the bitch's system may have a detrimental effect on the puppies. The effects of infection, live vaccines or injury to the bitch may either prevent the normal development of the whole foetus or cause deformity to limbs. It is thought that defects such as cleft palate or imperforate anus occur at this time and severely deformed foetuses may be reabsorbed by the bitch's system. At five weeks of pregnancy, the physical signs may be more apparent. There will be more development of the mammary glands and a slight bulge may be felt just behind the ribcage. The bitch's abdomen may feel hard and firm, although the enlargement of this area is only just starting. The nipples will be more firm and erect, but the most promising sign is the turning upwards of the hair of the lower abdomen. This is caused by the change of shape, but is more noticeable than manipulation. A white or pale-coloured discharge from the vagina is often noticed and this is a good indication of pregnancy. The discharge is not profuse, just remaining within the lips of the vulva or clinging to the immediate area. Any foul-smelling discharge or bloodstaining should receive veterinary investigation.

The bitch should receive an increased amount of food from this stage, by roughly a quarter of her usual quantity per week. Some bitches will become ravenous, others will accept the increased portions with less enthusiasm. It is very important that the diet is balanced. Increasing the carbohydrate in a mixed diet may satisfy the bitch, but it will do little to aid the development of the litter. The increased quantity of food offered must be a balanced mix. Adding meat only will increase the protein level, but is bound to cause digestive upset. Complete diets can be supplemented to make them more palatable, but care must be taken. Your Bernese bitch will probably appreciate her meals divided into two or three smaller helpings at this stage, as one larger meal may make her uncomfortable.

From six weeks of pregnancy onwards, the physical signs should be obvious if a good-sized litter is being carried. If only one or two puppies are present, then a bitch may keep her owners guessing for a week or two longer. As the foetuses develop and grow, there is little room for the uterus to lie normally in the abdomen so it folds back upon itself and moves, usually lower down into the abdomen. This can happen over a very short period of time, and the change in shape of your bitch will be dramatic. Some bitches experience some discomfort at this time and may cry out or go off their food for a day or so. As the weight of her now loaded abdomen is pulled down by gravity, her spine and haunch bones may be more noticeable. Viewed from above, she may look rather sunken on either side behind the rib cage, although rather bulbous lower down. A waxy secretion will appear around her nipples and this should be carefully cleaned away as it will attract dirt and dust. Exercise should not be too exhausting, and so a few short outings per day is much better than a long marathon once a day.

The maternal instincts of a Bernese bitch do not always appear at the correct time. Her instinct to prepare for a litter may occur at any time during the pregnancy, and it is likely that some digging for a likely nest will occupy her time. If a number of bitches are kept together, there is a possibility of some jealousy erupting into fighting for a few days. This may be instigated by the pregnant bitch or others who are upset by her condition and the smell of her discharge. Pregnant bitches, especially those who are almost full term, should not be left alone with others for long periods. Apart from the risks involved in the daily jostlings, she will appreciate a place of her own where she can seek seclusion. It is a good idea to introduce her to her whelping place now, so that she will regard it as her safe place.

From the seventh week of pregnancy your Bernese bitch should be fed as and when she demands. Some days she may be more willing to eat than others. This may be due to discomfort due to her size, weather conditions or to number of other reasons. But veterinary advice should be sought if she refuses to eat for a couple of days or more. I add a calcium supplement to the bitch's food from now and continue this until the puppies are weaned. The calcification of the puppies' skeletons will make a great demand upon the bitch's own reserves and this must be replaced. Some breeders also like to include milk in the diet, and I see no reason why this shouldn't be done as long as it doesn't cause diarrhoea in the bitch. Highly nutritious food should be offered to bitches on a mixed diet and the addition of cooked eggs, cheese and any other easily digested food will be appreciated. Those bitches fed on dry complete foods will have an increased thirst directly related to the high intake, and milk may be offered sometimes instead of water.

The average duration of pregnancy in the bitch is nine weeks but puppies can be born – and survive – from the fifty-seventh day. Owners should not be fooled into thinking that large-breed puppies need to be carried full term – they can and often do appear early, especially when a large litter is restricted by space in the uterus. At about seven-and-a-half to eight weeks of pregnancy, I like to trim the coat around the bitch's vulva and remove some of the coat forming her trousers to make cleaning easier after the birth. Bernese with a very profuse coat would benefit from the removal of some of the hair around the nipples. Not only will the puppies find suckling easier, but less dirt and wet will be brought back in to the puppies after visits to the garden. The hair between the pads and toes can also be trimmed to advantage for the same reason. A full coat can be maintained, and some bitches appear in the show ring very soon after the puppies are weaned. For those who have not reared a litter before, you will soon realise that your time will be very limited after the birth, and the time spent on washing and drying tail and leg featherings several times a day would be better spent on other chores. A shorter coat is easier to wash and dry than a long one, and showing must take second place to the well being of the litter.

PREGNANCY TESTS

Patience is really the one thing that most owners lack, and after the planned mating some people find it almost impossible to contain their enthusiasm for the much-awaited litter. Ultrasound scanning machines are now used to diagnose pregnancy in the bitch, but the facilities are usually few and far between. The method is used to diagnose pregnancy in sheep, and so some large animal practices may be able to help you. Veterinary schools and some independent businessmen can also provide the service by arrangement. The diagnosis is said to be ninety-four per cent accurate, and owners usually visit for two or more screenings.

A new blood test provided in kit form to your vet is now available and this boasts an accuracy of ninety-nine per cent in the period from twenty-eight to thirty-seven days. The blood is sent to a laboratory to determine the protein level in the blood and the results are known within two or three days. Although physical signs may already be appearing by this time, an anxious owner can be reassured and future plans can be made. If the tests prove negative, then those bitches who are engaged in a false pregnancy can avoid the production of unwanted milk, as their food intake can be limited and their exercise increased until the false symptoms are past. Veterinary manipulation can detect puppies in some bitches between the twenty-eighth and thirtieth day, although in a large breed which often carries puppies high, this is not always the case. Many bitches have fooled both their owners and professionals, and the only way to be 100 per cent sure is to wait and see!

Whelping Preparations
A utility room or conservatory is an ideal place to site the whelping box. If a bitch has lived as part of the family, she will be happy in such a place as she will have peace and quiet, but is also not left out of things completely. The whelping area should be well lit and ventilated. It should be warm in cold weather and cool in hot weather and it should also be draught-free. An electric power point to use for a secondary heat source for the puppies is necessary, and so is access to hot and cold water. If a spare room in the house is to be used for the bitch and her litter, then it is advisable to remove or cover carpets and mats, as they will become soiled as the bitch travels to and from the garden. Ideally, the owner should sleep close to the puppies for a few days, so room for a light bed is needed. I prefer to have a whelping box in the bedroom, as well as in a room next to the kitchen, so that the bitch and puppies can be watched during the night with minimum upset to the routine of the family and other dogs. But I know that many will feel this is unnecessary. All I know is that I have never lost a puppy after birth, and I would like to keep it that way. Once the first week is over, then the puppies are big enough to be uncomfortable to the bitch if she should inadvertently sit or lie on one, and she will also be more accustomed to her new duties and so more trustworthy.

The whelping box can be either a permanent wooden type or a makeshift one made of cardboard or disposable thin ply or hardboard. If breeding is to feature on a regular basis, then a good sturdy wooden whelping box which can be dismantled will be a valuable acquisition. Whichever type you use, it must be big enough for your bitch to lie, stretched out along one side, with ample room for the puppies to move away from the bitch if so desired. For a Bernese, the minimum size would be four feet by three, and ideally five feet square or five feet by four feet. The use of rails will make the lying area smaller, and this should be borne in mind by those who engage a carpenter to make one from a plan.

Most whelping box designs are for sides which are twelve to fifteen inches high. I believe this kind to be virtually useless, as puppies can easily climb up on to the side of a bitch and fall out of the box. Sides which are twenty-four inches high are much better, with access from a panel in the front as this can contain the puppies more easily. Such a box will prevent unwanted attentions from other dogs, and provide the bitch with a feeling of security.

The construction should be of exterior grade ply or marine type ply at least two centimetres thick. The front of the box should be a panel which can be removed completely for when the puppies need more space, and an access panel can be incorporated to allow the bitch ease of coming and going. For a bitch who needs to see what is going on around her, a small wire panel can be slid into the access hole enabling her to be secure, yet keeping her in place. The floor of the box needs to be raised off the ground an inch or two, and a removable shelf rail will give more protection to puppies than a pole-type crush rail. The box should be sanded absolutely smooth, and several coats of marine or exterior varnish should be applied so that cleaning is easy.

In an emergency, a cardboard construction can be useful, and of course it is cheap and easily replaced when soiled. This would need to be sited at the corner of a room so that at least two sides are supported, and ideally a third side so that the weight of the bitch against the sides will not distort or move it. The large cartons made for a television or a washing machine are best, or smaller ones can be tied together to form one large container. Access into one side is needed and hinges can be made with string. At least twelve inches of cardboard should be folded under, so that they will keep the sides in place by the weight of the bitch and her puppies.

Polyester fur pads, ideal for whelping, are also, I feel, essential for rearing a litter and for the comfort of your bitch. Not only does the "fur" provide an easy medium for the puppies to move about on, but all the wet and moisture from the puppies and the bitch will drain straight through on to a layer of newspapers underneath so keeping everyone dry and comfortable. The prolonged lying of the bitch as she nurses her litter can cause soreness, but this is completely avoided if she has this bedding under her. The bedding should fit the box exactly, or with a slight excess so that there is no chance of it moving or of a puppy becoming trapped underneath. The better quality polyester fur bedding has a very stiff backing, and this is far safer than the cheaper more flimsy type which will move about and form creases.

A huge stock of newspapers should be collected before the litter is due. Not only is it needed during the whelping, but also after the birth right up until the puppies are ready to go to their new homes. It is surprising how many will be needed and they are easily disposed of. Friends can be encouraged to save them for you and unsold copies can be bought from wholesalers. These are ideal for newborn puppies as they are free from contamination and will present little or no risk to the vulnerable babies. Newspapers which have been stored in an outbuilding may be contaminated by vermin or mould from dampness and are of no use to you. For puppies which are three-weeks-old or more, shredded paper which is available for horse bedding is wonderful for laying over newspapers, to keep puppies clean. Although soiled papers should be removed as often as one passes by, the shredded paper will be kicked over wet and soiled patches as the puppies move about and will stop them constantly becoming dirty with faeces and urine. Again, this is easily disposed of and can be stored without difficulty.

An extra source of heat may be needed for newborn puppies in very cold weather, or if the puppies are small and weak or orphaned. Heated pads which are placed on the floor of the box are less hazardous than overhead sources of heat. The pad should be sited towards one corner of the box, so that the bitch can lie away from the heat for her comfort. The puppies will converge on the covered pad quite naturally without any encouragement. Infra red heat lamps are still used by some breeders, but they do tend to have the disadvantage of causing dandruff on the puppies. Such a lamp, usually available from farming suppliers, can be hung over the corner of the box. The height will need to be carefully calculated as burning can occur.

A small cardboard box containing all the things that you may need during the whelping should be assembled ready for the event. Another small box is useful to put the puppies in as they are born, pending the arrival of the next. A small piece of the polyester fur bedding or an old towel and a hot-water bottle can be made ready here. In the other box, place the following:

Old towels for drying the puppies. These can be discarded afterwards if necessary.

Ten lengths of thick, strong thread for tying off any bleeding umbilical cords.

A container of surgical antiseptic and a pair of blunt-ended scissors.

A tube of lubricating jelly.

Two rolls of kitchen towelling (paper).

Two plastic waste disposal sacks.

Two lidded buckets. One for placentas which are to be discarded, another for any dead puppies.

A notebook and pen to write down the time of arrival of each puppy and the time between contractions. The vet will need to know this if the bitch experiences delay during the birth.

A large collection of newspapers to mop up the fluids that are lost during the birth. A piece of the polyester fur bedding can be used during the whelping, but if this is in short supply, a good thick covering of newspapers on the floor of the box will be adequate.

Finally, the attendant should have something to occupy the time while waiting for the arrivals. The bitch may be unsettled by the constant gaze of a worried owner, so if you can occupy yourself while keeping watch, then you and your bitch will be less stressed.

Is The Whelping Imminent?

The one sure sign that the whelping is on the way is the drop in temperature for the twenty-four to thirty-six hours before whelping. The normal temperature of a dog is 101.5 degrees, and this will fall to about 100 degrees for the last week of pregnancy. If the temperature is taken both morning and evening for the last week, the final drop to 99 or 98 degrees is easily noticed and so plans can be made. The first stage of labour may be heralded by long periods of restlessness or by complete calm. Frantic bed-shredding may occur, or this may only happen as the real pains of contraction occur. No two bitches are the same and for every bitch that seeks comfort and reassurance, another will want seclusion.

THE BIRTH

Whether or not the first signs of labour are noticed from the signs mentioned earlier, a sure sign is shivering in the bitch. Most Bernese bitches will spend a great deal of time licking and cleaning any or all parts of their anatomy that they find easy to reach in their enlarged state. If the bitch has been accustomed to her whelping box for some time prior to the expected birth, then she may be happy to spend her time there during the first stage. However, she may well choose to find a quiet and out-of-the-way place. The time taken over the first stage of labour is variable, and may be directly linked to the bitch's temperament. A rather humanised bitch may become neurotic about the whole procedure and react in a hysterical way for up to forty-eight hours, while a calm and steady bitch may go through this stage with hardly a sign. There may be a mucous-like discharge from the vagina and it may appear as being rather string-like, clinging to the hair around the vulva and featherings. This is the plug which has sealed the cervix, and it has dissolved in readiness for the birth.

Between bouts of shivering or bed-making, the bitch may sleep peacefully, only waking to begin the process again. Bed-making, either before the end of the pregnancy or at the start of labour, is thought to be prompted by the discomfort felt by the full uterus. As the first pains of labour occur, so the bed-making and bed-shredding intensifies. If the bitch is allowed to shred a good thick layer of newspapers placed ready in the whelping box, she may settle more easily having satisfied her craving.

At the first sign of labour, all other dogs and animals, as well as interested spectators should be cleared from the area, leaving one or at most two attendants who are well known and trusted by the bitch. An ample supply of clean water should be available to the bitch for drinking, and any trips outside to relieve herself should be carefully monitored. In darkness, she should be carefully watched and a powerful torch should be used to ensure that she does not leave a puppy outside. Some veterinary surgeons will appreciate a call to advise them that labour has started, and many owners get great comfort from knowing that the vet will be prepared if his help is needed. The way in which the bitch is managed through each stage of labour and the birth can affect her future attitude to motherhood. A highly-strung bitch who may panic during the pains of labour, needs to be told kindly but very firmly that she must not behave in such a way. Some bitches are perfectly capable of getting on with the task of producing a litter, but others will need to be managed very carefully for the benefit of all concerned.

THE SECOND STAGE OF WHELPING

This is the actual birth of the puppies and can only commence when the cervix is completely dilated. The bitch will have become more settled, except during the contractions when she may be rather agitated. Between contractions, the bitch may be settled, even trying to sleep. As the pains intensify, she may lie on her chest in a hunched position, she may sit against the corner of the box and brace herself as she strains or she may stand with her back hunched, turning to inspect herself from time to time. The puppies could be born in any of these positions, but it will kinder to the puppies not to let them drop to the ground if the dam insists on standing.

The function of the owner during the contractions is to ensure that everything which may be needed is at hand, and to comfort the bitch and be ready to take charge of the puppy when it arrives. Whelping is a natural process, but many bitches do not have the natural instincts to know what to do with a new-born puppy. Ignorance and clumsiness can result in stress to the puppy, so I prefer to take charge of the first few puppies born to a first-time mother. Not only will this avoid any regrettable mishaps to the puppy, but the bitch will relax and settle, so giving her some time to adjust to this new experience.

Watery fluid may also be lost from a ruptured water bag – the amniotic sac – and this again is quite normal, although it does not always occur. Any very dark or foul-smelling discharge, or any considerable loss of blood could mean a problem so veterinary advice should be sought quickly.

The sight of the water bag, which looks like a black balloon at the vulva, heralds the birth of the first puppy. The bag may appear and then retract or it may remain unmoved for some minutes depending on the strength of the expelling contractions. It is normal for the bitch to want to investigate this protrusion, but she shouldn't be allowed to bite at it. If the bitch seems to have a low pain tolerance, she should be firmly prevented from becoming too upset. Most puppies are expelled very easily, although the first-born may take a bit more time as it is in effect stretching the passages ready for the other puppies to follow. Occasionally a puppy may be partially retained, and a few strong contractions and strains may be needed before it is fully released. If a puppy appears to be stuck, and these are usually only those which are presented hindlegs first, a little help will bring about a happy conclusion.

About half of all puppies are presented hindlegs first, but this is not a real breech presentation. A true breech is when the rump is presented first with the hind legs tucked up along the stomach. There is no reason to think that puppies presented hindlegs first are not normal: they are as normal as those which appear head-first. A great deal of pushing on the part of the bitch is needed to expel the head of a puppy, and the rest of the body follows easily on a head-first presentation. Because we do not see exactly how many pushes are needed to expel the head, we do not worry; so there is no reason to worry when the body comes first and the head seems to be taking a few more pushes. A prolonged retention of the head can bring about some swelling or even brain damage but this is unlikely during most whelpings. A particularly large puppy can be difficult to expel, but it will come with a little human intervention. First, make sure you have scrubbed your hands and fingernails. Then apply a small amount of the lubricating jelly just inside the vagina, trying not to get any on the portion of puppy which has emerged. Using a rough piece of towelling, the puppy should be gripped firmly but gently and as the bitch strains, a simultaneous rotation and downward pull should free the puppy from the obstruction. It is useless to contact the vet for assistance once part of the puppy has emerged; valuable time is wasted, and the vet would be unlikely to attend in time to save the puppy. This is one of those situations which you have to approach in a sensible and calm manner.

Once the puppy is clear of the dam, you must decide on the best course of action. If the dam is calm and showing reasonable interest, then she can be allowed to take a more natural involvement with her first offspring, than if she is highly stressed. I think it is a good idea to free the puppy from the encompassing membranes as soon as possible, and only then allow the bitch access to her new baby. During the birth the sac containing the puppy may already have ruptured and it can be pulled away from the puppy's head and body. If complete, the membranes can be broken between the thumbs and forefingers, freeing the head first. Most often the placenta arrives with the puppy, but if it is still within the bitch, wait until she has another contraction to expel it and then help to ease it away from her. The puppy can still be freed from the membranes even if the placenta has not yet arrived. The expulsion of the placenta is regarded as the third stage of labour. A green staining from these membranes is quite normal and nothing to worry about.

The puppy, now free from membranes, can now be moved to the bitch's front to allow her to inspect it and hopefully recognise it as her own, and so a bond is made. The bitch will lick the puppy in an attempt to stimulate its breathing responses and the puppy may cry out. She may seem to be rather rough but as long as she is not hurting the puppy, do not be too concerned. The dam may instinctively eat the placenta, or afterbirth, which is still attached to the puppy by the umbilical cord, which she will also chew through with her side teeth. Inexperienced bitches may break the cord too short, and may try to pull the puppy about by the severed end. If this about to happen, then it is advisable to sever the cord with scissors after it has been tied off with thread. The blood which is visible in the cord should be eased toward the puppy between the thumb and forefinger and the cord should be ligatured about two to three inches from the puppy's abdomen. The placenta can then be offered to the bitch. The placenta would be the only source of nourishment to a bitch in the wild for some days after the birth of a litter. Even though our Bernese have long been domesticated, there is still great value to the bitch if she is allowed to consume at least some of the placentas. They are blood-filled, and consequently highly nutritious to the dam. They also contain hormones which will aid the let-down of milk into the mammary glands and help the uterus to return to normal size after the whelping. The drawback is that the bitch may experience black, watery diarrhoea if she consumes too many. If the bitch has a large litter, then she should only be allowed to eat about half of the placentas. Those discarded can be put into a lidded bucket and disposed of later. Occasionally a finicky bitch will refuse to even look at a placenta and no harm will come to her if she does not eat any of the afterbirths. Bitches who whelp by caesarean section rarely experience difficulties even though denied access to the placentas.

Once your bitch has had the opportunity to lick the puppy, then the attendant can rub the puppy vigorously with a piece of rough towelling. This will help the puppy to dry off, and also help stimulate the natural responses. The puppy's mouth should be checked, and wiped out with a folded sheet of kitchen paper to remove any debris. As soon as the puppy is dry it will be able to conserve body heat. Puppies usually protest loudly at the attentions of the attendant; so if the dam becomes worried she should be firmly but kindly pacified. A puppy which appears lifeless can be brought around by massage, and by helping the excess fluids which may be 'waterlogging' its system escape. Puppies which appear rather blue in colour will almost always respond to stimulation and rarely suffer ill effects. Vigorous massage with rough towelling, turning the puppy from side to side, should be alternated with swinging the puppy to remove the fluid. Hold the puppy's head between the first and second finger, keeping its body in the palm of the hand. With a firm grip, an exaggerated movement of swinging the puppy from shoulder height right down to hip level will expel some of the retained fluids.

Any puppy which seems to be breathing irregularly can be helped by massage and the application of heat. Holding the puppy on a warm hot-water bottle will help, or as a last resort the puppy's body can be immersed in a bowl of warm water. But this does have the drawback that body heat can be lost when it is removed for the massage to begin again. If there is any sign of life, perhaps just an occasional gasp with long periods of lifelessness, then there is good reason to continue stimulation. Puppies have been known to recover and begin to function normally after as long as thirty minutes from birth. If another puppy is about to be born, an assistant may have to take over.

After a prolonged delivery, it is possible that one or more puppies can be born dead. These pups usually appear very white on the pads, inside the mouth and around the tongue. Even so, a little time spent on massage may stimulate life, and so it is worth the effort. Anything can be tried, even artificial respiration. There is also a product available from the vet which is useful to have in an emergency. Made by Ciba Geigy under the brand name of Respirot, a few drops under the tongue will treat asphyxia of newborn animals and is often effective when all else fails. If the puppy is truly dead, then it should be wrapped up and removed from sight of the bitch so that it can be disposed of later if veterinary opinion is not sought.

As soon as the puppy is dry and breathing efficiently, it can be returned to the bitch and encouraged to suckle. Some puppies will immediately attach themselves to a teat and feed greedily, others may be less interested. A puppy does not need to feed straightaway, but suckling will help the let-down of milk, and it is also thought to help the birth process for the rest of the litter. The action of one or more puppies suckling will help the bitch to settle and accept her new responsibilities. If your bitch has whelped on polyester fur bedding, then the puppy will be able to grip and hold its position better than on newspaper, although a piece of towelling can easily be placed under the puppy to help it balance. Any puppy which seems disinterested or too weak to suckle can be coaxed by wetting the nipple and holding the puppy's nose just underneath, as puppies always nuzzle upwards in their search for a teat.

Whether suckling or not, the first-born can stay with the dam until the next arrival is imminent. Wait until the next puppy has started to appear before removing the first-born, or the bitch may worry. The first-born should be placed in the prepared cardboard box, and this should be kept either in a corner of the whelping box or just outside the box where the bitch can see it. Noisy puppies will settle down to sleep if they are covered lightly with a towel. In a natural situation this would not happen. But in the confusion of the second birth the puppy could be injured as the dam moves around to clean each new arrival, and each puppy would become wet with every new birth.

Only when the puppy is safely arrived and settled with the dam should the owner worry about logging down the time of arrival and any identifying marks. If there is sufficient time between births, the puppies can also be weighed: but the priority is to ensure that each puppy is well. Between whelping, each puppy can be checked for deformity, cleft palate, a condition causing a split in the roof of the mouth which prevents natural suckling, is common, and other defects occur occasionally. Once the second puppy has arrived safely, then the process is repeated and the first-born can join its new littermate at the teats. When the next arrival is about to make an entrance then the two can be removed to the cardboard box until it is safe for them to join puppy number three, and so the process goes on. When two or three puppies have been delivered, the dam may be allowed to take a more active part in cleaning the puppies, as she will have had time to accustom herself to her new experience. Her initial fears and confusion will have subsided and so there will be less risk of accidents with the puppies, and no doubt inexperienced owners will also have had time to impart more calm to the situation.

Between arrivals, soiled newspapers can be removed from the whelping box and replaced with clean, and the dam can be offered a drink of water. The temperature of the room should be constantly monitored. The puppies need to be warm enough, but the dam should not be so hot as to be uncomfortable or distressed. The behaviour of dams during whelping can vary greatly. Some will continue to scrape up the bedding in the whelping box with each new set of contractions; others will accept each new birth with scarcely a movement. The length of time between the deliveries can vary: some puppies arrive within a few minutes of the last, others may appear two or three hours later. Any bitch who is experiencing contractions for more than an hour without result may need veterinary intervention. A visit to the garden to urinate may get things moving along, but remember to take a torch and watch the dam closely in case a puppy should arrive outside. A bitch may sleep soundly between puppies, and this is no cause for concern as long as she is not distressed. There are no set rules. A litter may arrive very quickly or it may take twenty-four hours or more, but most owners will know instinctively if there is a problem.

WHELPING PROBLEMS

As each bitch is different, there is no way that anyone can lay down guidelines for dealing with problems. If in doubt, a veterinary surgeon should be contacted and his advice should be followed. I fail to see why novice owners ask for help and then refuse to take it. Firstly, I would like to reassure worried owners that if a veterinary surgeon requests a bitch to be brought to the surgery, he is not being thoughtless and unkind. Often, a ride in a car will promote contractions and so bring about progress in delayed whelping. If intervention is needed the vet has all the necessary equipment in the surgery, so time will often be saved.

Uterine inertia is probably the most common cause of whelping difficulties in the Bernese Mountain Dog. This can be caused by a number of factors, and inertia can occur at any stage during the whelping. Inertia of the uterus, simply explained, means that the muscles are not contracting correctly to bring about a normal birth. There are a number of causes for this: heredity, poor condition of dam or an over-stretched uterus. Primary inertia can occur when an obviously pregnant bitch fails to start the first stages of labour or goes through the bedmaking stages and maybe a few minor contractions but is then unable to complete the second stage of labour. A caesarean operation is often recommended in these cases.

Secondary inertia occurs when one or more puppies have been born, but the natural process of expulsion of the puppies slows down to a stop. This is often caused by exhaustion of the dam or fatigue of the muscles of the uterus. If the cervix is dilated, then injections of oxytocin may be administered. This is a hormone produced by the pituitary glands and will often induce a puppy to be born within about ten minutes. One injection may be all that is needed to get the remaining puppies delivered, but an injection may be needed to expel each remaining puppy. Injections of calcium may also be given to increase depleted blood calcium levels.

Over-sized puppies or puppies presented in a breech position occur only occasionally, and often there is little time to go for professional help if the puppy is to be saved. Most over-sized puppies will eventually make their exit if they are rotated to allow an easy delivery and this can be done by lubricating the internal passage of the bitch as far as the fingers will reach, after suitable scrubbing of course. Standing a bitch on her hind legs with her front legs held by an assistant will sometimes help with the force of gravity working for you both. Breech presentations, where the rump is presented and the hind limbs are tucked under the stomach, need to have the hind limbs brought forward before delivery can occur. Again, a well-lubricated passage is needed before the attendant can hook a finger around the puppy's stifles to bring about expulsion. If veterinary help is at hand, this may be done manually or if the puppy is higher inside the bitch, then forceps may be brought into use.

The appearance of a dark, foul-smelling discharge is an indication that something has gone wrong, and time should not be wasted in seeking advice and possible treatment. A thick, green discharge is sometimes in evidence when the placentas have begun to separate and disintegrate, and this should be a sign for immediate attention if the unborn puppies are to be saved. This discharge is not at all similar to the watery green stain which appears quite naturally at delivery. Apart from a few traces of blood which may erupt from the umbilicus of the newly born puppies, the dam should not lose any blood herself during the whelping. If blood is seen in any amount, this could be caused by the rupturing of minor blood vessels, or by the tearing of the vaginal tract. If bleeding should persist for more than a minute or two, then again help should be summoned. But remember, a small amount of blood will spread into a large area, especially on bedding that is already wet from the whelping, so be sure to gauge how much blood you see.

A caesarean operation is so common an occurrence these days as to be little worry to a

Bernese owner. Modern anaesthetic advances make the risk minimal to both dam and unborn puppies and most bitches undergoing such surgery show no problems afterwards. If a caesarean is advised before any puppies are delivered naturally, then the veterinary surgeon will usually provide a box and heated pad to receive the puppies as they arrive. If one or more puppies have been born at home, these should be left in a warm box, preferably covered to conserve heat, and they will be quite all right while the bitch is taken to the surgery for delivery of the remaining puppies. Paper towelling will be available at the surgery, but towels can be taken to speed up the drying process.

Watching a caesarean operation is a fascinating experience, and not at all the bloody or horrific sight which many owners fear. Most vets will allow owners to remain while they operate, but care must be taken to be unobtrusive. An extra pair of hands to receive the puppies as they are removed from the uterus will enable those slower to respond to be given more stimulation. Puppies born this way do not experience the contracting movements of the dam's muscles, and so they will possibly need more manual stimulation to breath normally. After surgery, the dam will recover from the anaesthetic very quickly, and it is not uncommon for bitches to walk out of the operating theatre. Once home, the bitch can be settled down with her litter, and will probably go into a deep sleep. The incision, which may have been made mid-line between her teats or on her flank, rarely causes difficulties and will heal surprisingly quickly. There may be a slower response from the dam to accept her puppies; but this is rare, and time and effort on the part of the owner usually result in bonding of the family.

After The Whelping

Once the final puppy has made its appearance, then both owner and dam can feel justifiably proud and a wave of relief will sweep over both. At least a couple of hours should elapse after the final puppy is born before you should assume that the dam is really empty. The dam's abdomen will of course be greatly decreased in size, and she can be made to stand while a gentle examination is made, by feeling along her belly with both hands. This will enable an owner to be confident that all the puppies have been delivered. If the number of placentas delivered relate exactly to the number of puppies born, then all well and good – although a retained afterbirth can be passed up to twenty-four hours after the whelping.

All the puppies can be placed in the cardboard box while the bitch is taken outside to relieve herself and the whelping box is cleaned and remade ready to receive the mother and family. It is not uncommon for the Bernese dam to be reluctant to leave her family to attend to her toilet needs, but she should be compelled to go with you, on a lead if necessary. Again, your management of her at this stage will be decisive in how easy or difficult it is for you to cope with her during the next few weeks. While the dam is away, the box should have all traces of the whelping removed and clean, fresh newspapers should be placed on the floor under the clean piece of polyester fur bedding. If a blanket or other kind of bedding is put into use, it must be of such a size as to fit the box exactly so that puppies cannot get trapped underneath.

If blood or fluid has stained the box, this should be washed off with a mild disinfectant. Beware of strong smelling cleaning fluids as these may irritate the delicate sensory membranes of the newborn puppies. Discarded placentas which were placed in the lidded bucket can be disposed of down the WC, and any stillborn puppies can be removed for burial or wrapped up in newspaper, placed in a plastic bag and if possible refrigerated, if they are to be examined by a vet. The temperature of the room must be constant, and a decision as to whether extra heat is needed for the puppies must be made. The heat pad or overhead heat lamp can be sited so that everything is prepared for the dam's return.

While the dam is safely occupied elsewhere, the puppies can be fully examined to be sure that none are deformed in any way. They can be weighed, and distinguishing marks can be logged if this hasn't been done already. Many owners are upset to find that puppies sometimes appear to have rather twisted hind feet, or feet which seem to resemble a clenched fist. This is not unusual, nor necessarily a problem. The condition can be caused by a number of factors, but in the majority of cases the feet function in the normal position once the puppies begin to stand, if not sooner. The presence of one or two extra toes on the hind feet can give the appearance of deformity, especially when novice breeders have only seen adults with four hind toes. The vet will remove these in a day or two without any problem. A variation in weight between puppies can occur, but this is no indication of final size. Lack of space within the uterus may be a factor, and if the dam was mated on more than one occasion, the puppies may not have been conceived at the same time.

Long or trailing umbilical cords can be shortened without fear of bleeding now, and some may have already started to shrivel. Each puppy should be carefully examined to check that all is well and that each is breathing and moving about in a normal fashion. The faeces passed by newborn puppies is a rust brown to orange colour and appears rather waxy. It may also appear to be rather more black in colour, but it should not be watery or passed as a foul-smelling puddle. The heads of newborn Bernese often appear rather shortened and wrinkled; this will change within a few days to a more recognisable shape. Once fully dry, the puppies will have a shiny coat, and if not fat already will fill out within thirty-six hours if they are feeding normally.

The white markings on Bernese puppies often appear to be broader than they will be upon maturity and the tan colouring seen on adults appears as a dark brown/black brindle, so do not be hasty to reject puppies as being the wrong colour. The white tail-tips and feet will be present; if not evident they will not appear later. The muzzle, lips and pads will often be pink, or even red with or without black pigmented points, this will change later to the full black pigment which is desired.

The question of culling is emotive, but it is a subject that must be considered. Occasionally a puppy will be born with some defect which will prevent it living a normal life. In these cases, the puppy should be kindly euthanised to save future suffering, and most people would have no qualms about making the correct and sensible decision. In Switzerland and Germany, Bernese litters are culled to a sensible number of six or seven puppies by direction of the breed club authorities. I daresay that this caused some problems in the early days of the practice, but nowadays the breeders have come to accept the situation, even though some will obviously feel regret and sorrow at the time. Right or wrong, it does limit the number of puppies reared, and it does go some way towards ensuring that a certain standard of markings at least is maintained for the breed.

In the UK as a nation, we seem to have the attitude that all life is sacred, even to the extent that I have known of puppies with cleft palates or even a limb missing being reared. It seems a strange world that congratulates breeders for rearing disabled puppies when there are literally thousands of dogs, of all breeds including some Bernese, which are looking for good, caring homes. It is one thing to have a genuine affection for an older dog which becomes disabled, and I am sure that we would all do everything in our power to maintain a high quality of life for an afflicted pet. But it is quite another to rear a defective puppy. It is true that many people may offer a home to a dog which they feel sorry for, but the temperament to make the right decision for both dog and future owner is an important requirement for a breeder.

If a large litter is born, there may be a reason to reduce the number. Some of the puppies may be very under-sized or weak, they may be poorly marked or badly constructed or there may be a shortage of homes on offer. These are all reasons to consider culling. I am sure most people would agree that it would be more upsetting to euthanise an older puppy or an adult for any of the above reasons. Veterinary advice should be sought, but breeders who have decided to bring puppies into the world, must bear some responsibility for their charges' future.

The Dam

While the whelping box and the puppies are being organised, the dam should have been taken outside to relieve herself and walk about to get the circulation in her limbs functioning after her time in the whelping box. She should have had access to water, but food need not be offered until she returns to her litter when she is more likely to concentrate on whatever she is offered.

The dam should be thoroughly washed down along her abdomen and down her rear with warm water and a sponge. A mild soap or shampoo can be used, but avoid strong disinfectants which may upset the new-born puppies. Dettol and Savlon liquid will leave a strong smell on the bitch which may distract the puppies from suckling, and it could be ingested by the bitch as she licks herself and puppies. Sterilising fluid may be safe, but unless the brand you have has been made specifically for the purpose of washing down dams after whelping, then it is best just to rinse the dam, once she is clean, with plenty of clear, warm water. The bitch should be thoroughly dried with one of the synthetic chamois leathers which are now available for the purpose. This removes all the water on her coat as if by magic. During the next two weeks the dam will need to be washed several times a day for her comfort, so anything which makes the job easier on her and you is a great bonus. Before the dam is brought back in to be reunited with her litter, she should be put on a lead and collar so that she is unable to rush in. She should be led into the whelping box and settled while under full control. This again will help set the pattern for her behaviour with her puppies, as she must learn to act carefully and steadily when near them.

The litter has arrived safely – but there is much work to come.

At three weeks old, the nose pigment is developing fast.   Sowerbutts

Place the cardboard box containing the puppies to one side of the whelping box and leave them in it until the dam has been settled down in the box. Only when she is lying down and comfortable should the puppies be placed near to her abdomen so that they can all be helped on to a teat to feed. If the litter is large, the dam must learn to lie completely flat to allow easy access to the lower row of teats. If the puppies need help to attach themselves, it is easier for the attendant to ensure that one puppy at a time is placed on a lower teat before the next row is filled. Puppies will hold on strongly if they have their front legs set high each side of a teat, and those on the top row will keep a firmer grip without wobbling if they are propped up between those suckling from the lower row. Smaller puppies may have difficulty in taking a large teat into their mouths; so this must be borne in mind even though the teats nearer the rear of the dam are often the most productive.

The puppies will make a paddling movement while sucking and after a while the milk will flow; puppies then do not have to work so hard, they just have to suck steadily and swallow. Many a novice breeder will marvel at the way the puppies' tails become erect and at the noisy gulping sounds that accompany the flow. One by one the puppies will go to sleep, some still attached to a teat for comfort. It is essential that all the puppies have an equal opportunity to suckle during the first two days of life, as the milk contains the valuable colostrum which contains antibodies to the diseases that the dam has encountered throughout her life, as well as a defence against those diseases for which she has been vaccinated. Therefore I would recommend that for the first few days the puppies should be placed near to the teats and encouraged to suckle every two hours. Smaller puppies may be pushed away from teats by larger siblings and so may be denied this benefit without owner vigilance.

Once the puppies have fed, the dam will want to lick and clean them. She will pay attention to their faces and stomach area, and will stimulate the puppies to urinate and pass faeces by licking. She will consume all the waste from the puppies for some weeks, and this is quite normal. Some bitches do become rather obsessive about cleaning puppies and those rearing a small number of puppies may have to be firmly discouraged from constantly soaking them. Although they are undoubtedly *her* puppies, a healthy respect for your wishes will not come amiss for the puppies and her own comfort.

Any puppy which fails to respond to the idea of suckling is not necessarily disabled. Some puppies do have slower responses for feeding. They should be kept warm and placed near to the teats and often the stimulation of the more lively members of the litter crawling about will create more interest. If a puppy seems particularly poor in getting the idea of holding on to a teat, it can often be induced to suckle if it is scratched quite firmly along the length of the spine in the opposite direction to the lie of the hair. I have found puppies will become quite agitated and cross, and if the teat is moistened they will usually take a grip on it for comfort if nothing else. The old idea of smearing the teats with honey does no more than present a possibility of the puppy getting a tummy upset through the sugar ingestion. Those puppies who are keen to feed but seemingly unable to find a teat need no more encouragement than a few drops of milk manually expressed and smeared around the nipple.

When the family is fed and cleaned, the dam may be offered a small light meal, although some bitches will refuse solid food for a day or more. White meat and boiled rice, cooked eggs or some similar, highly nutritious but easily digested food can be offered every four hours or so, followed by a drink if required. If the dam has been fed milk regularly, she may be keener to drink this than water but if she is unused to milk it may cause diarrhoea. Finicky bitches may be tempted by the liquid invalid diets sold in chemists for human consumption. Great care must be taken not to upset the dam's appetite by constantly pushing food at her. She must be encouraged to eat well as she will need a lot of sustenance to rear her litter. There is nothing wrong with tempting a finicky feeder with a few choice morsels, but the dam must be encouraged to eat sensibly if she and her litter are to remain fit. The addition of vitamin or mineral supplements may cause meals to be rejected, so consider the possible reasons if food is refused.

The dam will probably settle down to a good deep sleep, but there is no way that the attendant can do the same. While the puppies are so small and vulnerable, they could easily be killed by the simple action of the dam turning around or rolling over. It is essential that there is someone in attendance, certainly within earshot, until the puppies are big enough to crawl away from under the dam, if she should accidentally lie across them. If the dam is settled and lies contentedly, she should be turned over every two hours for her comfort. She should also be taken outside to relieve herself regularly, even if she doesn't appear to want to go, and of course, any discharge clinging to her hair and body should be washed away before she returns to her litter. The bitch will lose a discharge from her vulva for some weeks after whelping, first seen as a dark greenish-brown colour for about a day after the birth, then changing from a dark brownish-red colour to a paler red as it diminishes. The amount of discharge lost will vary according to the size of the litter as it is the residue from the attachment sites of the placentas on the wall of the uterus. If the discharge should appear black and foul-smelling, it should be investigated by a vet without delay.

With only a small number of puppies in a litter, a bitch can suffer from mastitis, and those bitches which have been particularly well fed are the most prone to the problem. The signs are one or more of the mammary glands appearing very reddened and very hot to the touch. The bitch may also show symptoms of fever and great discomfort, but this is not always experienced. First aid from the owner can give some relief before veterinary attention is available. A towel soaked in warm water and then wrung out should be applied to the affected area, and the milk should be expressed manually and discarded. Puppies should not be encouraged to suckle from this teat straightaway as the milk will be affected. Manual expression can be attempted every hour or so and after about four treatments the strongest puppy in the litter should be encouraged to draw from the teat. Veterinary treatment usually involves an antibiotic injection, and most bitches return to normal very quickly, although a close watch should be kept on the mammary glands throughout the weeks that she is feeding her puppies in case of recurrence.

The First Week

Newborn Bernese puppies will sleep about ninety per cent of the time during the first fortnight of life. They will only awake to feed and to be cleaned and as long as they are warm, they will be quiet and contented. Puppies which constantly cry out or which seem reluctant to respond to the attentions of the dam have something wrong with them. Puppies will sometimes become lost, crawling around to the back of the dam or even try to suckle from her vulva. You can help these puppies return to the area of the teats, but some are likely to be more mobile than others. It is quite possible for some puppies to crawl up over the flank of the dam and I have had several puppies like this in past Bernese litters. We always christen these mobile puppies true "Swiss Mounting Dogs" and we have discovered that in some cases they continue to develop as active adults. If the litter contains one or more of these mobile puppies, then the worth of the crush rail will soon be realised and appreciated. When newborn puppies stray from the dam, they will often sway their heads from side to side and even crawl in a circular pattern. It was once thought that they were trying to scent out the dam and so find their way back, but it is now accepted that these movements are in fact a signal to the dam to draw her attention to their predicament. The dam will respond by licking the puppy, and the puppy's automatic reflexes will compel it to crawl towards the dam's stimulation. Some Bernese bitches will try to pick up puppies and move them about, even attempting to bury them under the bedding if they feel threatened. Do not scold a bitch for holding her puppies in her mouth, but discourage her by distraction.

The puppies can be weighed daily and they should double their weight in a week. Puppies often lose an ounce or slightly more after birth or they may remain stable before weight is gained during the second to seventh day. A litter containing just a few puppies will obviously grow faster than puppies from a large litter. If there are more puppies than teats, it is essential that all puppies have an equal chance of suckling and the puppies should be marked in some way so that they can be alternated on the teats as the milk flows. Puppies with similar markings can be marked by a spot of nail varnish on the top of the blaze where it will disappear in time leaving no trace.

The dew claws can be removed by the veterinary surgeon any time after thirty-six hours after birth to four days, depending on the independent practice. If six toes are present on the hind feet, I prefer to have my puppies done at about forty-eight hours after birth as I feel that a much larger wound is made if they are removed after this time. Some vets refuse to remove hind toes, but ideally only four toes should be left on the hind feet. Front dew claws rarely cause problems in the adult as most Bernese have rather stumpy slow-growing nails but it is acceptable to have these removed also, if desired.

Dew claw removal can be done at home or in the veterinary surgery. If the dam is well and doesn't need to see the vet for examination, I feel it is better to take the puppies to the surgery while the dam is occupied at home. The puppies can be put into a suitably prepared cardboard box after the dam has been taken into the garden, and then taken off to the vet. The puppies will cry out loudly in protest as the claws are cut off, but they will soon forget the pain and settle within a moment or two. The wounds are sometimes sutured, but most commonly they are sealed by the application of Permanganate of Potash crystals (Potassium Permanganate) which stops bleeding almost immediately. I have found that cauterisation, the burning of the wound by a platinum-pointed cautery iron, can cause a delayed shock reaction and so I never allow this on my puppies. If a white absorbent paper has been placed on the bedding in the box containing the puppies, then any puppy who still has a bleeding wound will be easily found and this can be stopped before the journey home.

If the option to have the dew claws removed at home has been taken, then the dam must be taken well out of hearing while the puppies are being dealt with. This can cause problems on a small property, as it is not a good idea to take the bitch for a walk out of the boundary for risk of infection. Even a radio turned on very loud in another room may not mask the puppies' cries. Once the dew claws have all been removed, it is advisable to keep the puppies in the small cardboard box for about thirty minutes before they are returned to the whelping box. This will restrict their crawling movements which may open a wound, and also keep them huddled which will give both comfort and warmth which will minimise the shock. Once you are sure that the wounds are all sealed, then the puppies can be returned to the dam. Keep them in the box, which has been placed inside the whelping box, and bring in the dam with the minimum fuss. Settle her down, and one at a time put each puppy to a teat until they are all feeding. Stay with the dam and puppies, and while they are feeding, dissuade her from licking at their feet. The dam will know that they smell different, but once they have fed they will have taken on more of her scent and it will be less noticeable. If the dam does not pay too much attention to the puppies' toes, then they can be left with her. If she does worry at the wounds, the puppies should be put back into the cardboard box for an hour or two before they can stay with the dam again.

The toe nails, both back and front will need to be trimmed every three or four days as they will scratch the dam quite badly and make her very sore if they are left long. This is a job which will need to be done regularly until the puppies leave for their new homes, so even inexperienced breeders will soon become proficient. The nails on very young puppies are usually pale and opaque and so the quick, the blood vessel within the nail, can be easily seen and avoided. Only the very sharp tips of the puppies' nails should be removed. If the quick is cut, not only is it very painful to the puppy, but it will bleed profusely. Toe-nail cutting is easier if it is done when the puppies have just finished feeding and are less active or inclined to struggle. Many kinds of nail clippers are available for both dogs and people, and so what you use will be a matter of personal choice. The guillotine type of clipper does not give a clean cut when they have become worn, and the pincer type are difficult to handle for some people. Nail scissors are usually adequate for the nails of puppies up to about two-weeks-old, but after that the nails will be too hard for this method of shortening.

The puppies will receive all their nourishment from the dam for the first two or three weeks of life, and this means that the dam must receive ample nourishment of the correct nutritional value to keep both her milk production and her own physical condition at a premium. Meals should be offered about four times a day and drinks should be offered more frequently. The dam should be fed in the whelping box so that she will not worry about leaving her puppies, and then she can be taken outside to relieve herself before being settled with her litter. A written record of the eating habits and requirements of the dam, noting any changes of appetite, will prove useful in case of future problems.

Visitors should be limited to those who are familiar to the dam. Apart from the risk of her being upset and possibly feeling threatened, there is also a possibility of infection being introduced to the vulnerable puppies. The dam should accept the interest from all members of the family, but small children should only be allowed access to the litter under strict supervision. Other pets should be kept well away.

Week Two
The dam will have settled into a nice routine with the litter now, even to the point of being more content to leave them unattended without undue worry. There is no reason why the dam should stay with the litter all the time, and breaks of an hour or so will do no harm. After feeding, the puppies will sleep quite happily and may not huddle together as often as during the first week.

The wet newspapers on the floor of the whelping box will need changing more frequently as the volume of urine from the puppies increases. The polyester fur bedding will also need changing daily as it becomes soiled by the discharge from the dam and the dirt which she brings in from her visits to the garden. The puppies' nails will still need cutting regularly, and the temperature of the room must still be monitored to ensure comfort. At any time from the eighth to the fourteenth day, the puppies' eyes will begin to open and simultaneously they will begin to attempt to stand and try to walk. Bright sunshine or artificial lighting should be avoided as the puppies become accustomed to their new-found vision. The eyelids may open immediately, or they may take a day or two to open fully. Bernese puppies' eyes look dark blue in colour when first observed and the third eye-lid is sometimes prominent. The puppies will distinguish light and dark, but cannot see properly until they are between ten and fifteen days old.

As the puppies try to rise up on their very unsteady legs, it is important to ensure that they can get a really good grip on the bedding in the whelping box. Some puppies affected with Hypomyelinogenesis (Trembler) are detected at this time, by a bouncing movement more pronounced than in non-affected littermates. The shaking movements will become more pronounced each day, until a fast shiver becomes apparent. Veterinary advice should be sought if this condition is suspected. The daily weighing sessions will also give an indication if the development of the puppies is abnormal, as owners will have become used to the feel of the babies. With improved sight and movement, the puppies should be handled gently and carefully to accustom them to human attention.

The increased milk production of the dam may indicate an increase in food and fluid intake. The dam may still appreciate being fed in the whelping box, and towards the end of the second week it is not unknown for the more active puppies in the litter to be attracted to the smell of the food and even attempt to climb into the food dish to sample the contents. If so, I feel that the time to offer a very small amount of meat has come, but many puppies may not show this interest in food for another week or even longer. Generally speaking, puppies in a large litter are more likely to seek food earlier than those in a smaller litter who are more satisfied by their mother.

The wounds caused by dew claw removal should be healed over completely now, and as the scabs peel away a clean pink area of skin is revealed. The umbilicus will be healed over completely, and those puppies who may have a small hernia here can be recognised by a small protrusion of fat which appears as a slight swelling when the puppy is held upright. Lying on their back, the puppies will show no sign of this.

The black pigmentation of the nose and muzzle should be progressing well, although there may be a great difference between individuals in the litter. Lack of correct pigmentation can be caused by a vitamin or mineral deficiency, but it is a hereditary characteristic and may be slower to appear on puppies from some bloodlines. At about fourteen days, the puppies' ear canals will open and so they will experience clear sounds for the first time. The twitching and other movements which have been observed in the puppies before this have been involuntary muscle movements, not a reaction to noise.

Some worming preparations are now available for dosing puppies as young as ten to fourteen days old and these can be administered according to dose safely with little risk of problem to the puppies. I do feel that a puppy will be better off without these parasites, but at such a young age there is more likelihood of the dam eating the expelled worms as she cleans up her puppies. Great care should be taken to avoid this if possible, as the puppies will still need licking stimulation from the dam to urinate and defecate. Of course, worms passed by the puppies should be rendered troublefree by the worming preparation.

Week Three

The dam's milk production will be reaching its maximum and so her appetite will be enormous. Food should still be offered four times a day, as she may find it uncomfortable to take too much food into the stomach at one time. There is a risk of Eclampsia (also called milk fever) caused by the lowering of blood-calcium levels due to the increased milk production. I like to increase the calcium level added to the dam's food as a preventative measure. Signs of problems are a staggering gait and a strange look about the dam's eyes. The temperature is often found to be sub-normal, and the onset is fast. This is one of the very few real emergency situations when veterinary attention is needed very quickly, for calcium injected intravenously will bring about a rapid and complete recovery. Eclampsia has occurred quite often in Bernese bitches and will affect bitches in both good and poor bodily condition.

Any discharge being lost by the bitch should be decreasing rapidly, and overall she should be looking very well. Her coat should be shiny and she will give an impression of contentment. The weight of her very enlarged mammary glands may still contribute to a rather sunken outline, but she should have a good covering of flesh and should not look thin. The time spent with her litter will begin to decrease by choice and the puppies can be left for two or three periods of two hours twice daily. If, however, the puppies are repeatedly left for longer periods without their mother, they may begin sucking each other for comfort. You may already have noticed that even after feeding some puppies will remain attached to a teat and will draw upon it while sleeping. If they are deprived of this basic need, sucking littermates will be a habit which quickly establishes itself and will prove very difficult to cure. The dam should be allowed to sleep with the puppies, as they will need feeding during the night, but her visits during the day can be spaced out between the feeds which are now offered to the puppies by the owner. The signs that extra nourishment is needed are clearly presented in a number of ways. Crawling into the dam's food dish has already been mentioned, and while suckling at the dam the puppies will continue to paddle the teats even after the milk has flowed, in an effort to stimulate a further release of milk.

As their increased needs become apparent, the dam may regurgitate her food for the puppies and this should be prevented by keeping her away from the puppies for at least an hour after she has eaten. The puppies' first teeth will begin to erupt between fourteen and twenty-one days and so they will be quite able to taste a small amount of meat if it is placed in their mouths. There is no need to offer Bernese puppies a milky meal, as they are receiving this from their dam and no substitute milk will be so acceptable at such a young age. Good quality raw beef can be scraped or finely minced, or canned puppy meat can be offered as the first few meals, and a small ball the size of a hazelnut can be placed on the tongue as a first taste of what is to come. I have known many novice breeders who have offered large quantities of meat but this results in the puppies having upset stomachs. A small quantity, as suggested, offered twice a day for the first two or three days will enable the immature digestive systems of the puppies to become accustomed to the new food. Cereals should not be added to the meat at this stage as it will cause slower digestion and so should be added only gradually over a number of days. A week after the puppies have been introduced to meat, they will be able to take about one ounce three times a day, feeding from their dam in between times. It is not uncommon for one or more puppies to be less interested in food than their littermates. This should give no cause for concern as long as these puppies are developing and gaining weight normally. A very small or underweight puppy may be rather backward in developmental terms, and such puppies should be encouraged to suckle from the dam as long as possible before they are introduced to meat with the rest of the litter.

The puppies will have been content within the whelping box for the first two weeks of their lives, but as they become more mobile they will need more room to move about. Unless the weather is exceptionally warm, I feel that puppies should be kept inside until they are at least three-weeks-old, as they chill very easily. The front of the whelping box can be removed and the area can be extended by the addition of rigid wire panels. The polyester fur bedding can be reduced in size and the puppies should have access to a good thick layer of newspapers which they will very soon learn to use for toilet purposes as their natural instincts will take them away from the bed to defecate. A wired in pen will give the puppies the opportunity to become aware of new sights and sounds, so preparing them for all the changes which they will experience during the next few weeks.

The puppies will begin to find their voices towards the end of the third week, and they will also try to bite each other in a very clumsy way. It is absolutely fascinating to watch them during this stage of their development and signs of individual character will emerge. Handling by people is very important now, and the more time spent with the litter, just holding and talking to them, the better they will react to humans in future. Bouts of activity will be followed by long periods of sleep, and it is during the sleeping times that the shape of the head and overall appearance is most easily seen.

The tan colouring will be clearing through nicely now, to a rather paler hue than seen on adults. The black coat will begin to take on a thicker appearance, and the presence of slight waves may indicate a possibility of a curly coat when adult. The bone on the front legs will seem thick and strong compared with the size of a puppy, and the feet will look large and rather flattened. The puppies' heads will now appear more Bernese-like, and those with broad heads at this age rarely lose this quality later. The bump above the nose is clearly visible, and often more prominent on males than females.

WEEK FOUR
The development of the puppies can be noticed daily now, as they become more independent of the dam, and more interested in their surroundings. Bernese puppies will now be recognisable even to a novice as the colouring and coat length is more like an adult.

A difference in coat texture will now be apparent, and those with a shorter coat or those that will develop a curly or wavy coat can be easily recognised.

The digestive system of the puppies should be well accustomed to the small quantities of meat which have been offered and so more substantial food is now due. Meals should be offered often but only in small quantities. The gradual change from mother's milk and meat to moist, soft, easily digested foods cannot be hurried, though most puppies will accept their new diet greedily, as they are burning more calories in energy as they explore and play with one another. The actual food which is offered comes down to owner choice, but I feel that puppies are more encouraged to eat a meaty-smelling meal than a bland complete food. Finely minced meat can be mixed with boiled white rice for a few days, then brown whole rice can be used. A great variety of puppy-grade meals are available, and these can be soaked before mixing with the meat.

Canned puppy meats are always readily accepted, but there is one drawback which many breeders have experienced in their litters. After passing through the puppies' digestive system, the waste is excreted in a very similar form to its original state, and inexperienced puppies are sometimes tempted to eat it a second time.

I have found that long, narrow, shallow dishes are the best for this weaning time. The dish can be placed along one side of the whelping box or pen, so that the puppies cannot walk straight through it. The puppies can be lined up with just their faces in the dish, giving them less opportunity to tread in the food. A piece of plastic guttering, with fitted ends is excellent for a weaning dish. It can be easily and cheaply obtained from a building supplies merchant. It is strong, yet easy to wash, and any length can be bought according to the number of puppies in the litter. The curve of the guttering will not trap food, and is at just the right height for the babies to feed from. Round, conical puppy feeding dishes are offered for sale at many pet shops, and these can be useful although they are very expensive and of limited use as the puppies grow.

Strict hygiene must be observed while the puppies are feeding, as some will urinate or even defecate in the dish during the process. It bears repeating that small puppies should never be left unattended with food. They may get food stuck to the roof of the mouth and so begin to retch. They may get a congealed portion stuck in their throat, or one or more puppies may not succeed in eating any food at all. Small puppies, once they have been active around the food dish for a few minutes will often curl up to sleep. If covered in food, they will become cold and upset, so they must receive attention during this time.

If the dam is still producing milk, the puppies can be allowed access to her after each prepared feed or between times, alternating meat meals with mother's milk. Puppies may require water to drink now, although any food offered should be very moist. A heavy bowl which cannot be tipped over is necessary for water, and until the puppies are five-weeks-old not more than one inch depth of water should be in the bowl. Again, a natural learning process of walking through the water must be experienced by every puppy several times before they understand that there is a distinct art in drinking without getting themselves wet.

While the puppies are eating, the dam should be kept well out of the way, as her scent

Four week old puppies will begin to play and investigate.

Five week old male puppies of uneven size and markings.

may distract the puppies. As the dam spends more time away from the litter, she will pay less attention to washing and cleaning them when she is with them. She can be pressed into service to help remove some of the food from the puppies' coats after they have fed, but she will not clean up their excreta so often, now that they are eating solid food. This is helpful when the puppies have been wormed, and of course the dam should be kept away from the puppies' toilet area after they have been dosed to prevent her ingesting any expelled parasites and also to allow you to see how infested the litter is. Worming preparations vary greatly, with new products constantly appearing on the market. I think that those preparations which dissolve the parasites in the puppies' gut may well suit squeamish owners, but I prefer to know if, and how many, worms have been passed. Dosing with worm pills or syrup should not affect the puppies' digestion if the instructions are carefully followed and the owner pays more attention to removing soiled newspapers on these days. The dam should also be dosed for worms with the same preparation and at the same time, depending on your vet's advice.

Once puppies have eaten a meal, they will appear rather fat and consequently they will collapse into a deep sleep. There is a temptation to allow puppies to sleep for long periods and then feed them again on demand. This is not a good idea at all. Feeding times should be regularly spaced to help their digestion. Once woken, puppies will need to urinate, and should be allowed a moment or two for this before food is placed in front of them. They will not need to be stimulated to urinate by the dam any more, the bladder and bowel being completely functional.

Bernese puppies will need regular handling to get them used to people, and if this is neglected at this stage in the puppies' development, there may be permanent temperamental effects later in life. Human integration is essential, whether your Bernese puppies are destined for a life as household companions or as working dogs. Complete human trust and respect is absolutely necessary in a large breed of dog, and Bernese are so dependent on human company that any puppy deprived of a full education will be bound to suffer later.

Grooming sessions for puppies must be frequent and thorough, not only to help keep the coat in good order, after all the washing following the messy feeding times, but to accustom the puppy to being inspected and examined. There can be few things more embarrassing than struggling with an adult or even a half-grown Bernese being presented for a veterinary examination, and so the sooner the puppies realise that such examinations are normal, then the sooner that a pattern for future behaviour is established.

The puppies should now have access to a puppy playground, which should be sited outside if the weather is nice enough. A safe area of garden should be enclosed with strong wire fencing, and if there is a possibility of draughts or a through wind, one or two sides should have a solid barrier to stop the puppies becoming chilled. Plants, stones and anything else which may prove harmful to the puppies should be removed before playthings are provided to help the puppies acquire skills. If grass is unavailable, then paving or concrete can be covered with a thick layer of hay to prevent the puppies from hurting themselves on the hard surface. Straw is unsuitable, as it breaks down into very small pieces. It is also rather shiny and will not absorb any wet or mess left by the puppies. Hay remains together much better and can be easily removed and disposed of on the compost heap. Puppies will play roughly from now until they go to their new homes, so some sort of cushioning is needed in their play area. Shade in sunny weather should also be provided if the puppies are to spend prolonged periods outside but four-week-old puppies should never be left outside if there is any risk of even the slightest shower of rain.

Apart from toys for amusement, certain articles can be provided to help the puppies with the skills of balance, coordination and mental adjustment. Only items which will not disintegrate from the attentions of the puppies should be considered, and these should be checked regularly for safety as the puppies grow and become more destructive.

The effects of rearing a litter may be seen on the dam, although many Bernese bitches if well cared for will look in the peak of health. As her milk supply is not now the sole source of nourishment to the puppies, her feeding regime should be planned to start to diminish her production. Some dams will already be producing less milk, especially if the litter is large, but those feeding just one or two puppies may be at the peak of production. It is quite safe to reduce the quantity of food, although not the nutritional value, offered to a well covered bitch who is still producing a lot of milk, and she can be allowed less frequent access to feed her puppies. Those bitches who are lacking in bodyweight should still be fed extra food, and again, limited access to the litter will prevent her from increasing her output. Any vitamin supplements should certainly be continued, and as she spends less time with the puppies she may be allowed to exercise more on safe ground where the risk of infection which could be brought back to her litter is minimal.

By this stage most Bernese bitches are happy to leave the care of the litter to the owner, but some may be anxious about leaving the puppies. Extra love and attention is needed for any bitch who is suffering from these very real withdrawal symptoms, and when she is not with her puppies she should have as much human company as possible. If other dogs or pets are in the household, these will be interested in the puppies, and protective jealousy from the dam should be avoided. You may know that other pets offer no threat to the litter, but the dam does not, and fights could occur. Even the most easy-going bitch may change character when she has a litter, so do not take chances.

Visitors may now be allowed, and the puppies will gain valuable experience from seeing and hearing different people to those they have been reared with. If your family lacks children, then carefully supervised visits from sensible children will help the puppies become accustomed to the erratic movements and high-pitched voices of these little people. Children should never be allowed to pick up the puppies, as wriggling puppies are easily dropped, and children cannot be expected to foresee danger. The risk of introducing infection when more people are allowed access to the litter is obviously increased, so you should be careful with your choice of visitor and then keep a close watch on the litter for signs of illness. Dogs, other than those within the household, should not be introduced to the puppies.

Advertisements offering the puppies for sale can now be placed, if the owner intends to sell locally. There may have been the opportunity to advertise the litter in a breed or specialist publication earlier, but it is not really sensible to advertise the puppies too early. The majority of purchasers will want to visit the puppies as soon as possible. The puppies are not really ready for viewing, and certainly not for choosing, until about five-weeks-old at the earliest. The owner's enthusiasm to sell should not put the puppies at risk of fear or infection. In local newspapers, as much information about the breed should be given, as well as the price. Non-Bernese owners will not be impressed or influenced by the names of the parents, but they will want to know if the puppies are well marked, house or kennel reared, and most importantly of all, how much they are. Countless wasted calls can be avoided by stating the price, as those not prepared to pay will be put off from calling. In breed publications, advertisements can be more specific with regard to bloodlines, health status of both parents, show wins, and anything else which may be relevant to those interested in the breed.

Week Five

The whole puppy-rearing routine should be well-established by now. The puppies should be eating well and regularly and the visits from their dam should be decreasing rapidly, their main purpose being to alleviate her discomfort as her mammary glands fill. There is more time involved in caring for the puppies, but there is infinitely more pleasure gained from watching them, and playing with them as they have become proper little Bernese, with individual characters and personalities.

The puppies will be more involved in play activities, and so daily grooming cannot be neglected. More time spent talking to the puppies should be an integral part of these grooming sessions which allow a one-to-one relationship to develop. Nail-clipping will still need to be done about twice weekly, as nails can do great damage to puppies during play. If they are allowed to become too long, the stance of the puppy will also be affected, and this is not conducive to correct muscle and limb development.

The paperwork which will accompany each puppy can now be considered, so that everything is ready for their departure. Canine insurance companies will supply a free book of insurance cover notes which can be sent for, and pedigree certificates should also be ordered from addresses to be found in the weekly canine press or from a stand at a dog show. The pedigrees are time-consuming to write out and it is easier to get them photocopied. An interim diet sheet can be mapped out, so that any prospective purchasers will have some idea of the kind of foods they will need to buy. The actual amount of food being given at the time of sale can be filled in at the last opportunity. A list of breed publications and addresses of breed clubs will be useful to puppy owners, along with a guide to the purchase of grooming tools, types of collar and lead and suitable toys. Advice about inoculations can be written down, although this may vary from vet to vet depending on which vaccine company they deal with. If the weather is poor, then a large area under cover must be provided for play during the day, even if the puppies are restricted to less space at night. For those who do not have or do not wish to use a kennel and covered run, the garage can be pressed into use.

When prospective owners respond to your advertisements, they can be invited to visit at a mutually convenient time. When they arrive, they should be introduced to the mother of the litter away from the puppies, as she may resent their attention to her precious family. Some time should be spent talking about the breed and its care before the puppies are shown to the visitors. Bernese puppies are so adorable that people fall in love with them, and your words will be lost on the entranced visitors. All the litter can be viewed, but they should not be over-handled, so a little tact with the visitors may be needed.

Prospective purchasers will need to be questioned as to their suitability to own a Bernese and this will involve all the skills of the breeder. Some people will be more than happy to tell you their life history with little prompting, others may be less forthcoming. As the breeder, you must try to establish as many details of the kind of life which is offered to one of your puppies before you commit yourself to the sale. There is an endless list of the kind of questions which can be asked; some breeders are more fussy about the kind of homes they seek for their puppies than others. The best piece of advice that I can offer is follow your own instincts. Even if all your questions have brought forth the desired answers, if you still have a doubt, back out! I have given people the benefit of the doubt in the past, and in most cases I have eventually been proved right in one way or another. Of course, every breeder wants to see the puppies they have so carefully bred and reared placed into homes at the optimum time for readjustment. But it is better to be left with one or more unsold puppies than to have them go to homes which are less than ideal. If a puppy is returned to you at a later date, it will probably need to be retrained and socialised extensively before it can be found another home, and of course each change of home is bound to have some effect on the dog.

If your visitors seem suitable, you may be happy for them to make their choice of puppy straightaway. If it seems that one half of a couple is less enthusiastic about the breed than the other, or maybe you have some doubts yourself, then give the visitors as much written information as possible, advise them to discuss matters for a day or two, and then to contact you again by telephone. This gives everyone a breathing space in which to make a considered decision. Once a firm booking has been made, it is a personal decision whether to ask for a deposit or not. Some prospective purchasers consider this to be a gesture of good will, and feel happier that the chosen puppy really will be theirs. Some breeders feel that a deposit shows commitment from the purchasers, but whether or not the deposit will be returned if the buyer backs out before a set time limit must be agreed. Breeders can be left with a puppy which was thought to have been spoken for, but this is preferable to the puppy being purchased so as not to lose the deposit.

Week Six

Now is the time to increase the daily time spent on educating the puppies. In small groups of two or three, the puppies should be introduced to the kitchen and previously unexplored areas of the garden to start to accustom them to unfamiliar sights and sounds. The puppies will get some reassurance from their littermates, so resist the temptation to remove the puppies singly for this first venture into the unknown. Only after this routine has been followed for a few days can the puppies be taken to explore on their own.

Singleton puppies can be introduced to new areas accompanied by their dams, but if the dam accompanies two or three puppies at a time, the puppies are more likely to be interested in the mother's milk, which is likely to have been out of bounds recently. The puppies surely can learn a lot in the company of their dam, but as they are soon to be on their own, gradual separation will help them adjust to their new homes quickly.

It is quite natural for the puppies to be chastised firmly by their dam for taking liberties. Humans seem unable to correct wrong-doings and to revert within a moment to a happier frame of mind, but bitches do just that with their offspring. Puppies will learn much more quickly from a sharp snap from the mother than from the constant nagging so often given by owners. We might all learn more about how to train our dogs if we observed natural canine behaviour more closely. When the litter is playing, wrestling matches will develop into heated arguments or even fights, and as quickly as they started, peace will be restored and everyone will play happily together again. This is all a natural process, and each puppy must learn to integrate with the others peaceably. If one particular puppy always seems to be the aggressor, then he should be firmly discouraged and reprimanded. A permanently submissive puppy should be protected from bullying. The temperament of individuals can be noted now, for instance, those submissive members of the litter quite happy to offer their throat and under-belly areas to more dominant members of the litter, older dogs and indeed humans. Puppies which resist human restraint for more than a moment or two or those which appear to be indifferent to human company will usually continue these traits in older life, unless they are subjected to an intensive behaviour training plan. Of course, puppies at such a delicate age will react more favourably to human commands on some days and seem totally oblivious to your existence on other days. Observation of these behavioural traits will help you decide on the suitability of individual puppies to the homes on offer.

The feeding of the litter should have developed into an easy routine, and with proper caution in view of the possibility of upsetting the puppies' digestive system, the introduction of varying foodstuffs can be attempted in preparation for any changes which they will encounter in their new homes. The puppies will probably enjoy chewing on a large marrow bone, which will not only help their teeth development and chewing skills, but will also be a useful pastime. With added weight and strength, the puppies' toys must be checked regularly as they will soon succumb to unfair wear and tear.

The dam will have finished feeding the puppies now, or very nearly so. In preparation for the massive moult which she will undergo in about seven weeks, she should have a carefully balanced diet and extra grooming and exercise to maintain good condition. She has undergone many changes, both physically and in her daily role over the past few weeks, and may be rather confused at the rapidly changing events. With so much time and attention focused on the litter, it is possible that the dam takes secondary importance as the departure of the puppies draws near. The puppies would not have come into being without the dam, and she may influence potential purchasers; if her temperament and condition is less than ideal, then it can be assumed that all may not be well with the puppies in the future. Therefore the dam should be a shining example of all that is good in a

Bernese, and she should be prepared for viewers just as much as the puppies. The pups will have left dirt and soiling on her coat, and although she will no doubt have cleaned herself, I find that my bitches really appreciate a good bath to set themselves on the road to normality again. It is important not to bath a bitch too soon after the litter, especially if the puppies are still feeding from her, as shampoo residue can cause sickness in the puppies if they ingest it. The coat must therefore be rinsed thoroughly.

The puppies may benefit from a bath now, as their eating habits, and playful antics are bound to leave their coats dirty. If they are bathed with a mild shampoo and are reassured while being blow-dried afterwards, they will be accustomed to the process which they will experience several times during their lives. I do feel that it is always nice to bath puppies just before they go to their new homes, and earlier bathing will avoid the shock of a completely new experience just before departure. The younger a puppy experiences this routine, the more easily it is accepted. After bathing, an anti-parasitic spray can be applied, taking great care to avoid the eyes and face of the puppy.

Week Seven

In the last few days before the puppies are old enough to leave, the breeder has a last chance to ensure that everything is ready to accompany the puppies as they go to a bright future. Diet sheet, pedigree and breed literature should all be in order, and the insurance cover should be ready for finalisation. Any specialised foods or puppy milk formula should be packed in small quantities to accompany each puppy to avoid major food changes in case owners have been unable to find a supply. This is also the last opportunity to introduce the puppies to anything which may be encountered in the near future, within reason. Extra attention to the regular habits of the litter will ensure that as many details as possible can be relayed to the new owners. The day before the puppies are due to leave, they should be bathed and groomed, and nails should be checked in case they are in need of a further trim. Dirty ears can be cleaned, making sure that details of any preparations used are written down for new owners.

The day that the puppies are to leave for their new homes, they should not be given a large meal just before they travel, as sickness will occur. Collection early in the day is advisable, and so a light breakfast can be offered, with more substantial meals to follow once they have arrived at the new home. Plenty of time must be allowed to talk to the collecting owners, and assurances to maintain a lifelong interest in the puppy should be repeated.

Whether or not the dam will be upset, or possibly even relieved, to see the puppies leave in the hands of strangers must be assessed by you, the breeder. Whether the rearing of the litter has been a new experience to you or not, it is all too easy to be so ensnared by the daily chores that you may forget to enjoy the experience. Puppies are adorable and none more so than Bernese. Breeding is certainly a serious business, and heartache as well as joy can be the result; but to all those breeders who produce Bernese puppies as a hobby, it is without doubt the most rewarding aspect of all canine activities.

CHAPTER THIRTEEN

Hereditary Defects, Ailments and Diseases

MOST dogs are bound to be affected by health problems at some time during their lives. Bernese are no more nor less healthy than any other type of dog, but some complaints are met more often than others by owners of this beautiful breed. The most important aspect of health care is the services of a really good veterinary surgeon. His qualifications should, of course, be above question, but he must also be someone that you can converse with easily. Some vets are rather awe-inspiring but it is vital to build a good relationship with your vet, and have the assurance that you and your dog represent more than just financial security to him. All vets are required to provide full round-the-clock emergency cover, so treat him with respect and only call him out of surgery hours when absolutely necessary, pay his bill promptly and you are likely to be rewarded with many years of good service.

In the event that first aid is needed, a kit can be kept at home in readiness for emergencies. It should contain the following essential items, and replacements should be purchased when items have been used.

FIRST AID KIT
Disinfectant – TCP or Savlon liquid
Cotton bandages
Crepe bandages
Lint
Cotton wool, cotton buds
Roll of adhesive plaster
Acramide wound powder
Antiseptic cream
Kaolin tablets or liquid for diarrhoea treatment
Plastic syringe for medicine
Scissors, tweezers, thermometer

The list of items could be longer but these are the most likely things you will need to deal with emergencies or minor problems. The syringe can be obtained from your vet. It is so much easier to give liquid medicine by this method rather than struggling with a spoon. The thermometer should be the round-ended type suitable for rectal insertion. The normal temperature for a dog is 101.5°F (38.5°C), and a rise of two degrees Fahrenheit should be considered serious. The temperature of a Bernese is easy to take, but an assistant should hold the dog's head to stop movement. The thermometer may be lubricated with a little vaseline and should then be inserted about two inches into the dog's rectum, after it has been shaken down to ensure that the mercury has fallen. Two minutes is the required time to wait, and you should keep hold of the thermometer while it is inserted in the dog in case he should eject it. After reading, clean off the thermometer, but not by rinsing it under the hot water tap, shake it down again and replace it in its shockproof case.

A detailed note of all treatment and illnesses of your dog should be kept up to date. If ever you needed to contact another vet in an emergency, these details could prove invaluable.

ARTHRITIS

A common complaint in both old and young Bernese. Arthritis is an inflammation of a joint, resulting in pain which may affect locomotion. The symptoms may ease once the dog has moved around for a while, but old dogs may tend to be reluctant to rise after sleep in anticipation of pain. Efficient painkillers are available for dogs, and surgery may be an option to alleviate discomfort. There is no cure, but the quality of life can be greatly improved for most cases.

BLEEDING

Most dogs will injure themselves at some time during their lives, resulting in the loss of some blood. Minor injuries may result in a small quantity of blood being lost and this will arrest naturally with no further problem. Blood has the unfortunate habit of spreading into pools of oceanic proportions when only an eggcupful has been lost. There is nothing more likely to evoke panic in an owner than the sight of blood from their pet. Minor cuts and abrasions can be cleaned with warm water and TCP and then dried with cotton wool. If the dog keeps licking at the spot, then application of neat TCP will often deter the dog as he will dislike the smell.

Bright red blood which seems to spurt from a wound will indicate that an artery has been damaged, darker red blood which seeps from an injury is coming from a vein. In both cases place a pad of lint, woven side towards the dog, on the injury site. Then add a good thick pad of cotton wool which has been immersed in water and squeezed out, and hold this in place firmly with a crepe bandage. Hold the pressure pad in place for at least ten minutes before pressure is lifted. If the blood seeps through, replace the cotton wool only and re-bandage. If the bleeding stops within twenty minutes, you can simply re-dress the wound, but with prolonged blood loss, and depending on the cause of injury, veterinary attention should be sought as soon as possible.

COPROPHAGY (Faeces eating)

Considered as unacceptable by Bernese owners, this habit can be very difficult to cure. There are many theories as to why it occurs, dietary deficiencies, food malabsorption or boredom, but none of these have ever been proven. Dogs engaged in this habit can be just as healthy as those who have never eaten their own stools, so the problem comes down to an inability for owners to accept the situation. The diet fed to the dog should be examined to ensure that it contains all the nutrients and food value needed by the dog and the possibility of hunger should be considered. If all is well here, then behaviour modification is the only hope of bringing about a cure.

All faeces left in the garden should be removed immediately and the dog should be scolded if he shows interest in his stools. Owners will need to supervise the dog's toilet habits to prevent the habit and on walks the dog should be kept away from fouled areas. Boredom is the common cause and dogs left unattended for long periods can easily adopt the behaviour. Some food types will produce faeces which smell more attractive to dogs than will other diets and it has been reported that a portion of raw courgette added to food will produce faeces with an odour found unattractive to dogs. Anything is worth a try but vigilance to prevent the action is the only way to avoid the habit.

DISTEMPER

In this age of effective vaccination programmes, Distemper is rare although not unknown to occur in recent years. It is caused by a virus infection, which can be complicated as secondary infection follows. Dogs contract the disease by breathing in particles emitted by affected dogs. Symptoms appear after seven to twenty-one days from contact and a temperature followed by discharging eyes and nose is noticed. Diarrhoea also occurs and some dogs have fits. The common name of hardpad came about because of the change in structure of the skin on the nose and feet. Nervous signs may never be lost; some dogs retain a twitch during later life.

Intensive nursing is needed to bring about recovery, together with antibiotic treatment. This may need to be changed during the course of the disease as different symptoms arise. Careful choice of antibiotics to treat infected puppies must be made to avoid permanent yellowing of teeth. Although no vaccine is one hundred per cent effective, the condition has dramatically reduced in incidence due to responsible owners ensuring that their dogs are inoculated. Breakdowns in the immune system have been known to happen among Bernese, and several young dogs have been lost to the disease.

DIARRHOEA

Most dogs will experience this at sometime during their lives and the most common cause is dietary, although it is a symptom of many illnesses. If the condition lasts for more than forty-eight hours, further investigation is needed. The natural colour of normal faeces will vary depending on the type of food being used and so too will the consistency. Some dogs' stools will be less formed when dry diets are fed regularly and so this should not be considered as true diarrhoea. Liquid faeces may vary in colour but if more than about a teaspoonful of red blood is passed, then veterinary attention should be sought immediately as this could indicate haemorrhagic enteritis which needs rapid attention. The first aid treatment for most instances of diarrhoea is withdrawal of food for twelve to twenty-four hours and quite often no further treatment is needed. Reintroducing easily digested foods to the dog will help avoid any further damage to internal tissue. Young puppies may become dehydrated, as can older dogs, so water should be freely available even if food is withheld. Persistent diarrhoea needs further investigation, as it may be an indication of many serious illnesses.

EAR MITES

Bernese seem prone to ear discharges, commonly referred to as canker, which are often caused by ear mite infestation. The dog is first seen to shake his head and scratch at his ear and initial inspection may show nothing seems to be wrong. Within a few days, the ear canal will become reddened and hot, with a dark red-brown waxy discharge in evidence. The dog will certainly resent inspection of the ear. Ear mites live their life cycle within the ear canal but they can be passed from one pet to another. The female mite lays her eggs in the warm, humid environment and so the cycle continues. Confirmed diagnosis of ear mite infestation can be followed by treatment which will be effective in perhaps about eighty per cent of cases, but some dogs who have had the problem for some time may always suffer from it to a greater or lesser extent. Proprietary medications are on sale which claim to alleviate the condition and in many cases these will be effective, but veterinary surgeons will be able to prescribe a more effective treatment.

The ears should be cleaned each day before any preparations are administered. The waxy deposit will prevent the medication from being fully efficient, and so as much of this as can easily be seen should be cleaned away with cotton buds. Never probe into the ear canal that is out of sight, as great damage, not to mention severe pain, can result. Cotton buds can be dipped into warm water to help loosen the waxy discharge, but spirit-based ear cleaners should never be applied to areas of broken or damaged skin. A free passage of air, as far as can be made possible, will help prevent future infestation, as will regular cleaning of the ear. Excessive growth of hair in the ear itself and around the inner ear flap can be trimmed away to advantage as an extra precautionary measure.

ECLAMPSIA (Milk fever)

Symptoms of Eclampsia represent a true emergency and delay in seeking veterinary treatment could prove fatal for the bitch. Decreased levels of calcium cause the bitch to become very restless and lose co-ordination so that the gait is staggered, and she will finally collapse into a coma. Those bitches rearing a large, demanding litter are at most risk, but any bitch drawing from her own resources to nourish a litter can be affected. It is seen occasionally before whelping, but it is usually when the dam's milk production is at its highest, when puppies are about two to three-weeks-old, that she seems most at risk. Even those bitches receiving calcium supplementation can be affected, so owner vigilance is essential post whelping. Recovery is both spectacular and fast after treatment. Calcium and glucose is injected intravenously and subcutaneously, and a calcium supplement added to food will normally prevent a reoccurrence, although relapses do occur very occasionally.

NB: Over-supplementation with calcium during pregnancy is thought to actually increase the likelihood of a bitch experiencing Eclampsia.

ECTROPION

The eyes appear reddened and may have a watery discharge but discomfort is obvious. The eyelids roll outwards, so that the conjunctiva is exposed so allowing entry to infection.

Disease of the cornea and conjuctiva is likely. Most often just the lower eyelids are affected and this ailment is seen increasingly in the Bernese Mountain Dog. An inherited condition, some dogs are in more discomfort than others, according to the degree of the defect. Surgery can alleviate the pain and discomfort of those badly affected, but this should not prevent breeders from working to eradicate the problem. The desire to breed dogs with small, deep set eyes is thought to be a reason for the increased incidence. Those affected should never be bred from.

ENTROPION

The opposite condition to Ectropion, Entropion involves part or all of one or more eyelids rotating inwards causing the eyelid and lashes to irritate the cornea. Prolonged contact will bring about ulceration of the cornea and so severely impair sight. A watery discharge is usually first noticed and upon inspection the eyelid can be gently rolled outwards by the fingers, only to invert again upon release. The dog will probably resent inspection – it is a very painful condition. Consider how a human reacts if irritated by just one stray eyelash or a speck of grit in the eyes and then think what this must be like when our dog is irritated by many lashes permanently.

Thankfully, a simple surgical operation will bring about some relief, but a growing dog may need several operations to correct the inward rolling as his head changes shape. Temperamental changes due to pain and frustration have been noted, and any affected dog should not be bred from as the condition is inherited. Modern surgical techniques can be successful to improve the quality of life for affected dogs, but should never be considered as a mask to allow the defect to be perpetuated.

GASTRIC TORSION (Bloat)

This is one of the few real emergency situations and delay in seeking veterinary treatment for the dog may prove fatal. The first sign that something is wrong may be anxiety and an inability to settle shown by the dog. The abdomen may not appear enlarged, but it will feel taut and hard and the dog will resent inspection. The abdomen will continue to enlarge quite rapidly causing some dogs to panic and they may even attempt to vomit or defecate. The dog should be prevented from drinking and movement should be limited. Speed in contacting help is of the utmost importance and a trip to the surgery for an abdominal operation is necessary.

The swelling of the abdomen is caused by fermenting food and an accumulation of gas in the stomach. The stomach may twist (torsion) and if this happens then both its entrance and exit are effectively blocked, so preventing evacuation. Breathing may also be impaired due to panic and the unusual pressure on internal organs. Surgery can be effective in bringing about relief but the condition can reoccur in future. Certain feeding habits have been implicated as likely to increase the risk of bloat, and so larger breeds who are most commonly affected should follow a carefully planned feeding routine. Large dogs should be fed twice daily to avoid overloading the stomach with one large meal; large quantities of foods known to be slowly digested should be avoided; drinking after meals may be delayed

Entropion: photo taken two days after surgery.　　*Haematoma: Buttons are sewn to the ear flap to stop fluid accumulating after surgical draining.*

for thirty minutes or more and exercise should be allowed only after one hour has passed after feeding.

HAEMATOMA

This is a collection of blood, a blood blister, that can occur at the site of an injury or blow. They most often affect the ear flap of Bernese, and sometimes cause little discomfort to a dog. But it may cause irritation resulting in constant head shaking and scratching. Haematomas can be treated surgically by opening and draining the blood, and the blood is prevented from accumulating a second time by suturing buttons to the outer ear flap as a means of exerting a steady pressure. If left alone, they will decrease in time, although there is some risk that the site may be punctured.

HEATSTROKE

Heatstroke can arise not only in hot weather conditions, but also after great exertion or stress. Leaving dogs in cars even in merely warm weather can be fatal to the unfortunate pet. In an enclosed space with limited ventilation, the temperature can rise alarmingly fast and breathing difficulties will soon arise. Some dogs will panic in such a situation, others will just become lethargic and even comatose. The immediate first aid measure is to bring down the temperature of the dog as fast as possible. Immersion in water, perhaps a stream or river, spraying with water from a hose or even packing the frozen foods from the deep freezer around the dog can be tried. Care must be taken not to bring the temperature down too far, and ten minutes of cooling is usually enough to enable the dog to be taken to a vet if one is not on hand. After an attack of heatstroke, it is not uncommon for the dog to be rather lethargic and out of sorts for some days.

HEPATITIS (Canine Viral Hepatitis, Rubarth's Disease)

A highly contagious virus, contracted by ingesting any substance soiled by infected particles. There is no connection with hepatitis in humans. Puppies under one year old are most at risk, but any dog can contract the virus. Generalised depression, lack of appetite, paleness of the gums, increased temperature and abdominal pain may be followed by jaundice. There is an incubation period of up to seven days, but the illness can appear rapidly, even resulting in death. Treatment can relieve discomfort of the symptoms, but the virus may be passed via the urine for some months after the symptoms disappear, and some dogs may prove to be carriers throughout their lives. Vaccination will give good immunity for the majority of young dogs and boosters throughout their lives may also be needed.

HIP DYSPLASIA (HD)

Hip Dysplasia, in its severe form, can inhibit the function and movement of affected dogs. It is a progressive disease and so its effect is increased in later life. A multifactorial condition, it occurs in many breeds, chiefly those weighing over forty pounds upon maturity. The hip joint is a typical ball and socket joint and deformity of either the head of the femur or the socket, or both, can impair efficient function. In Bernese, those dogs which will experience difficulties moving will often show the first signs of deformity between the ages of four and seven-months-old as both size and activity levels increase. Puppies with HD will be disinclined to run and play as much as normal puppies, and so a calmer temperament is observed. Reluctance to rise from a lying position may be noticed and once up the puppy will exhibit the classic sawing movement. At every opportunity the puppy will sit down. As the deformity progresses, there is obvious muscle wasting of the thigh and around the stifle (knee) area and when standing, the puppy will set his hind legs forward in an effort to take more bodyweight on the front legs.

It is quite obvious that the quality of life is impaired, but many affected Bernese do gain mobility as muscle development builds up around the ill-fitting joint in time. These dogs which have shown symptoms at a young age will never be cured, but they will most likely live a happy and pain-free life until the inevitable effects of arthritis call for further veterinary treatment. Surgical removal of the femur head is successful in reducing pain for those dogs so severely affected that euthanasia is the only other alternative. Cutting the pectineus muscle also relieves pain and allows much greater freedom of movement in about seventy-five per cent of cases.

Hip Dysplasia incidence needs to be reduced because it causes lameness and crippling to varying degrees in some dogs. It is true that some dogs function well and may show no indication of the condition other than upon X-ray, and this is why all breeders of breeds which can be affected should have all breeding stock X-rayed and scored to evaluate hip status. Radiographs for Hip Dysplasia evaluation are easily organised and involve a very simple procedure. The dog presented for X-ray is immobilised by anaesthesia or sedative and then laid on its back. The hind legs are extended fully and rotated inwards to allow the clearest picture of the joint. Correct alignment of the joints is necessary for an accurate reading and X-rays of dogs in the incorrect position should be rejected. In Switzerland, a second position is employed for X-ray diagnosis, and this is the frog position with the hind legs pushed up into a crouching position and rotated outwards. These radiographs are then graded or scored by specialists and the dog receives a permanent classification. In the UK and Switzerland these X-rays can be done at any time after the dog is one calendar year old. In the USA, a permanent grading is made after the dog is two calendar years old. As the hips are likely to wear as the dog grows older, the age of X-ray evaluation may be significant to obtain the best hip status certification.

Hip Dysplasia follows a pattern of genetic predisposition with outside influences affecting the seriousness of its effect. A puppy with this predisposition who is reared sensibly with little trauma may show minimal signs of the defect, another may be grossly affected. The growth rate and feeding regime of families of dogs has been monitored, and this research has shown that these factors definitely affect the onset and progression of the disease. In Switzerland and Germany, there are strict rules governing which dogs can be used for breeding, and hip status is regarded as very important. Only those dogs with 0 or 1 grades are allowed to enter the gene pool. This ruling has meant that the incidence of the condition has been reduced over the years but it is debatable whether the defect can be eliminated completely. In other countries without such controls, breeders can use which dogs they wish, but if an excellent Bernese with less good hips was used it would hopefully be mated to a compatible type but with a good hip background and possessing good hips itself. Hip Dysplasia is important as it does cause pain to some dogs. However, we must be sure not to place so much emphasis on one defect that others are allowed to become established within the breed. Breeders must always be aware that there are a number of defects which need to be reduced in incidence; those diseases which cause pain must be high on our priority list for attention. But a reasonable attitude must be adopted to ensure that the good qualities of the breed are retained as we work towards reducing faults.

HYPOMYELINOGENESIS (Trembler)

In 1986 there were reports of the birth of some Bernese puppies who began to show symptoms of Hypomyelinogenesis. In fact, the first diagnosed case in the breed was in 1983 when an eleven-week-old puppy began to tremble. As time went on, there were more puppies born showing similar symptoms, and in 1986 a meeting was held between the committee members of the British Bernese clubs and a veterinary and genetics expert from the University of Cambridge Veterinary Department. The symptoms of the disease become apparent at ten to fourteen days old as the puppies begin to learn to stand and walk, when they exhibit a characteristic bobbing up and down motion and the trembling is very exaggerated. Soon the trembling becomes very rapid so it is not so easily seen from a distance, but when the puppy is held it can be easily felt. As the dogs grow older, it is known that the condition can remain constant, or it can be progressive. Some dogs are affected more seriously than others, and the onset of symptoms can be much later than already mentioned.

In simple terms, the condition is caused by a lack of myelin – the sheath of insulation material which covers the nerves of the spinal cord. In effect, the nerve impulses do not travel directly to the desired place, getting spread out along the way so causing the involuntary trembling. There is no known cure, and the disease has been found to be a recessive hereditary trait from the evidence to hand. The condition has been seen in other breeds, and other species are known to suffer from inadequate myelin and similar symptoms caused by both inherited and virus factors.

In the UK, it seems that Duntiblae Nalle is the dog that appears as the common ancestor and geneticists' findings implicate him as the first known carrier. The disease may have started by a mutation of genes or Nalle may have inherited his apparent carrier status from one of his parents. As far as we know the condition has not been recognised in Bernese in other countries or from Nalle's close relatives. It appears that line breeding to Nalle has meant that the chance of carrier animals being mated together has increased the chance of affected puppies appearing. Of course, no one knew that this dog was producing carrier offspring, so no one can be blamed for the condition, or for the fact that there are many, many carriers now within the breed. These can only be identified as such when they are mated to another carrier and one or more affected puppies are produced. Geneticist's advice is that recognised carriers should not be bred from to maintain the breed, although they may prove useful to act as test-mates to clear other dogs and bitches. Carrier Bernese are normal themselves, and do not show any indication of being a carrier. To understand how the condition has been disseminated through the breed, the percentages over a large number should be as follows.

Carrier mated to another carrier will give on average 25 per cent affected, 50 per cent carrier, 25 per cent clear

Carrier mated to clear (unrelated) will give on average 50 per cent carrier, 50 per cent clear

Clear mated to clear will give on average 100 per cent clear

The trembler gene in the affected trembler Bernese has to come from both parents; a common ancestor or ancestors must appear on both sides of the pedigree. Recognised carriers are still being used and even if mated to a complete outcross, carriers will still be produced. There are many carriers, many unrecognised, within the gene pool in the UK and offspring from some of these carriers have been exported. If any of these exports are carriers, then they too are producing carrier offspring and so the condition can appear in other countries as it has in the UK. Of course, there are also clear dogs being bred, but these are not going to increase the problem in the breed. Bernese which are unrelated to Duntiblae Nalle are not implicated. Out-crossing Nalle descendants will avoid the production of affected puppies, but carriers will still be produced if one parent is a carrier. Individual breeding practices will have to be decided upon, and of course there are many aspects of the breed to consider when planning a mating. Those unwitting breeders who produced carriers or affected Bernese before the condition was recognised as being of inherited origin are blameless, but those who knowingly increase the carrier population without good reason should perhaps have their motives questioned.

KENNEL COUGH (Infectious Canine Tracheobronchitis)
A number of viruses and bacteria are involved in producing several strains of kennel cough which means that immunity to one or more strains will not prevent the symptoms occurring. The virus is carried in airborne particles, so risk of infection is greatly increased when large numbers of dogs collect, but single pets also contract the disease. The summer usually brings about an increase in numbers affected, caused to some extent by the mixing of dogs in boarding kennels.

Symptoms are a throaty cough, which may begin as an occasional throat clearance, and soon progresses into harsh, persistent coughing. Dogs rarely look ill and most will remain happy with good appetite and an unaffected daily routine. A slight discharge from the eyes may be noticed, and tonsilitis can occur in some individuals. Infected puppies may develope pneumonia complications. Antibiotic treatment is usually very effective, and some owners dose with an expectorant cough linctus to ease throat irritation; honey will also soothe a sore throat. Infected dogs should not mix with others for at least six weeks. A vaccine is available to give protection against one of the commonest bacteria known to cause the symptoms, and this is administered as nasal drops. Boosters are needed after six or nine months.

LEPTOSPIROSIS
Two forms of the disease can affect dogs, both of which can be passed on to people. One form is acquired by contact with dead vermin, or rat urine which has contaminated water, food, or the ground, and so farm dogs are at greatest risk. The second form of the disease is passed from dog to dog, most commonly via lamp-posts or sniffing urine in exercise areas. Symptoms in both cases include fever, diarrhoea and possibly some blood loss, excessive thirst and increased urine output, and ulceration of the mouth. The first form also shows jaundice, and there may be permanent kidney damage in the second form. Nursing of affected dogs should be done with great care to avoid owner infection. The virus is excreted in the dog's urine for some months after recovery, and so the risk to both people and other dogs should not be ignored. In man, the condition is known as Weils disease, and often proves fatal if treatment is not sought quickly. Vaccination of puppies, with booster injections for adults, must be considered essential.

MASTITIS
Inflammation of one or more of the mammary glands of a nursing dam can be noticed soon after whelping or possibly much later. It is the posterior glands which are most often

affected and they are very hot, very hard and extremely painful to the bitch when touched. The milk in these glands will be discoloured or even blood-stained, and the puppies will avoid suckling from the affected glands. The bitch may also show signs of fever, listlessness, and possibly refuse food. Application of warm towels, and expressing the milk at regular intervals will bring about some relief, but antibiotic treatment is usually required. As the condition improves, the strongest puppies in the litter should be encouraged to suckle from the teats that were affected to prevent a recurrence. Bitches rearing a small litter should have their milk production regulated by careful limitation of food intake. Over-production can cause congestion in the glands, and if the excess is not taken in by the puppies, problems are bound to occur.

METRITIS

After a whelping, bacterial infection can occur in the uterus. It can result from a protracted or difficult whelping, unhygienic conditions or possibly the retention of placentas or other foetal membranes. The acute form usually occurs within about a week of whelping and the signs are a putrid and often blood-stained discharge from the vulva coupled with fever. Bitches try to ease the discomfort by assuming a crouched position bearing weight on elbows and hocks. The production of milk may be reduced and the dam may show disinterest or even resentment to her litter.

Antibiotic treatment will ease the condition, and a full recovery can be expected in most cases. The puppies may have to be reared alternatively during treatment of the dam. Manual assistance during the whelping may introduce infection via the bitch's vagina, so scrupulous attention to hygiene must be observed. A hormone injection given to the bitch after whelping will ensure that the uterus contracts normally and that any retained membranes will be expelled. The mammary glands should be kept free of discharge deposits which may encourage the growth of bacteria.

OSTEOCHONDRITIS DISSECANS (OCD)

This condition occurs in many animal species and in the dog is commonly seen to affect the shoulder, elbow, hock and stifle joints. The shoulder seems to be one of the most common sites in the Bernese Mountain dog and puppies up to one-year-old are most likely to show symptoms, although the condition has been diagnosed in older Bernese who had previously shown no symptoms of lameness. Foreleg lameness can be caused by a number of things and it is important to remember that some lameness is caused by simple injury.

The ends of the long bones do not ossify – turn into bone – until growth is complete. During growth, these bone ends are formed in cartilage, and the term Osteochondrosis means quite simply that there is degeneration of this cartilage. The cartilage becomes thicker than normal in the absence of ossification, and cracks can occur. A flap can form from these cracks, or pieces can break away forming a joint mouse. Because the flap is not made of bone, it may not be seen easily upon X-ray, but the change on the surface of the area can be seen, so the condition can be identified. Lameness may be constant, but it may also come and go if a joint mouse is present – it is the movement within the joint from the floating mouse which causes most discomfort, some times more than others.

The most common time for lameness to occur is between five and eight months of age. Usually only one foreleg is noticed as lame and rest may improve the condition. But it will reoccur when normal exercise is resumed. Muscle wasting may be noticed on the affected leg and when resting there will be little weight on the leg. Strangely, manipulation will rarely cause obvious pain to the dog. Treatment can vary, but once correctly diagnosed the lameness will rarely improve without surgical correction. The affected joint is opened and loose particles are removed, following which a few weeks rest will often give complete soundness. The opposite leg to that showing lameness may also be affected, and so this may need surgery, although not always.

A survey carried out in the UK gathered information on some 1200 Bernese, and the information was sent to Dr Heather Pidduck at the University of London Royal Veterinary College. Her findings were most interesting. A higher percentage of males were affected than females, and the overall impression was that the faster-growing dogs were more at risk. OCD does tend to occur in related animals and so some genetic influence may occur. Cases were noted from most bloodlines, but some lines seemed to produce a higher incidence. Rearing and management also plays a part, especially when siblings share not only the same genes but also the same environment. The summary of the report recommended the following.

1. Breeders should feed and manage for slower, steadier growth.
2. The inheritance of OCD appears to be high, and so this could be changed by selective breeding.
3. Do not breed from those affected dogs and bitches, even those sound after surgery.
4. First degree relatives should be avoided, as these may be transmitting predisposing genes.
5. In-breeding on affected stock should be avoided.
6. Breeders should keep full and accurate records of all stock bred, and so in future a greater understanding of the condition may be gained.

As a final note, affected dogs can lead a normal and active life, but everything should be done to reduce the incidence of the condition. Careful management of youngsters during the crucial growth stages will minimise the risk of lameness in one or both front legs, and if lameness does occur veterinary treatment should be sought without delay.

PARASITES
Even those dogs kept in the cleanest conditions can become infested with parasites during their lives. A vast array of parasites exist, but those most commonly contracted are mentioned here. Parasites fall into two main categories: Ectoparasites which live on the skin and Endoparasites which live inside the body.

Ectoparasites
The most common is the FLEA and most owners will have seen at least one of these little charmers, indicating the presence of literally hundreds. The flea lays its eggs on the dog's

bedding or in carpets and warm crevices around the house, where the larvae hatch after two to fifteen days before entering a pupal stage to reach full maturity in seven to ten days. Hatching can be delayed by low temperatures, which explains why there is always increased infestation after warm weather spells. Fleas can be difficult to see on a dog, but they are easily noticed if they run across the white muzzle on a Bernese. Sight of the flea droppings on the dog's skin may be the only indication that the dog is harbouring these insects. These droppings look like hard black grains of sand.

Some Bernese are tolerant of flea irritation, others can react severely, causing large patches of allergic dermatitis. Many owners have reported that their Bernese have caused great areas of hair to be lost by constant licking at sites of a flea bite, resulting in large areas of ulceration. Regular treatment with anti-parasitic preparations are essential to prevent and treat infestation, even in single-dog households. Extra care should be taken to treat dogs after swimming and bathing and before encountering other dogs at shows. Confirmed infestation should also indicate thorough treatment of the house and all likely areas as well as the dog's bedding. Dog and cat fleas cannot live on people, but they will stay on long enough to bite and cause discomfort.

HARVEST MITES are sometimes known by the common name of Chiggers, and these are barely visible to the naked eye and are most often seen on the earflaps and between the toes as a minute red particle. The mites burrow under the skin to feed, causing great irritation to the dog. The infested area may become blistered before a scaly area develops, and owners often consider that an allergic reaction is causing the symptoms. The natural host of these mites is the field mouse, and so those dogs with access to their habitat are most at risk. Treatment is by veterinary-prescribed preparation.

TICKS lay their eggs away from the host animals; once hatched the larvae climb on to vegetation where they await the passing of a suitable host. Areas in which deer and sheep are allowed access are usually those places where dogs are likely to collect one or more of these passengers. The tick larva attaches itself by its head to the dog and feeds upon the blood until it is so engorged that it may resemble a bean in size and shape. Many dogs seem unaware that they have a tick feeding from them, but some may react by constantly biting or scratching at the site.

The tick should never be pulled off, as the head will remain within the dog and cause an abscess. It is essential to remove the whole insect and this is most easily achieved by drenching with surgical or methylated spirit on a swab of cotton wool to loosen the hold and then carefully easing the insect's head out of the skin. Where several ticks are present, veterinary help may be needed. Preparations to prevent infestation are commonly applied in anti-flea treatments, but special washes which should be left to dry on the coat are also very effective.

CHEYLETIELLA species are small parasites which burrow under the skin, and are commonly known as walking dandruff because of the scurf produced by their presence. This dandruff most frequently appears on the dog's back, but can be seen on other sites of the body. The insect is so small as to be barely visible, and once under the skin it can be very difficult to detect. Consequently, careful application of treatment to remove both adults and eggs from the dog is required to ensure that the long life cycle is prohibited from continuing. Cheyletiella can also cause severe irritation to people, especially children and those with sensitive skin.

Endoparasites

ROUNDWORM (Toxocara Canis) can infect both adults and puppies. There may be physical signs of ill health which indicate their presence, but in adults especially they may be tolerated without indications. Puppies with a large infestation have a characteristic pot-bellied appearance, staring dry coat and overall appearance of poor condition. Diarrhoea may be present, and a ravenous appetite enables enough food to be eaten but this fails to increase body flesh and improve condition. Puppies become infested with roundworms because they are born with larvae, passed to them from their dam, while in the uterus. By two weeks old, these have developed into mature worms, which will go on to lay eggs in the intestine. Older puppies and adult dogs will become infected with worms by ingesting eggs passed out in faeces and these eggs are able to live for many months on soil and vegetation before continuing the lifecycle in the new host.

Roundworm eggs may be picked up by humans, but more at risk are children because of their play habits. Eggs, once swallowed can develop into larvae in the human gut, but they will not continue to grow into adult worms. The larvae can migrate around the body, and in most cases no ill effects will arise, but occasionally one of the migrating larvae will settle in the eye so causing some loss of vision. Puppies should be wormed thoroughly before they leave the premises of the breeder and at regular intervals during puppyhood and adult life. Puppies are likely to reinfect themselves more often than adults, and so they should be wormed more frequently than the three monthly routine for all adult dogs.

TAPEWORMS, (Dipylidium Caninum) live in the small intestine of the dog and can grow to a length of almost two feet. The head of the worm attaches itself to the wall of the intestine, and each segment of the body contains eggs. When these segments are excreted by the dog, they dry out to look rather like cucumber seeds, or perhaps large grains of flattened rice. They may be found sticking to the hair of the anus. The incidence of Tapeworms in pet dogs causes general lack of condition in adults, and sometimes retarded growth and diarrhoea in puppies. Fleas act as intermediate hosts for tapeworm: the flea swallows eggs passed from the dog, and if a dog inadvertently swallows a flea, the worm larvae will mature into adults in the dog's intestine. Regular worm treatment should be undertaken, especially after a dog is known to have been infested with fleas. Tapeworms can, although very rarely, infect people and children are once more at greater risk.

Parvovirus

A disease only known to exist in dogs since 1978, its appearance was both widespread and spectacular. Virus particles are excreted by the dog in faeces, and infected dogs may contaminate footwear, clothing and other objects. Extremely resistant, disinfection is rendered very difficult, and the virus can remain active for up to a year. Two forms are seen in the dog, Myocarditis and Intestinal.

Newly-born puppies which have not received immunity from their dam are most at risk from Myocarditis. The virus will centre on the heart of the puppies, as this is where the cells are multiplying most rapidly. Damage to the heart muscle may not be apparent until the puppy grows and becomes active, and so puppies are liable to collapse and die without prior warning between the ages of four and twelve-weeks-old. All puppies in the litter may be affected to some degree and those who may have been exposed to the virus should be examined by a vet to determine if any heart damage is present.

Intestinal Parvovirus will affect any age of dog from four weeks to old age. The first signs are depression, vomiting, and the passing of a foul-smelling watery diarrhoea, sometimes containing blood. Dehydration and collapse commonly follow, and treatment must be applied rapidly as dogs can quickly succumb and die. Recovery may be complete, but digestive problems may be encountered throughout life. The symptoms are commonly treated by fluid replacement to counteract dehydration caused by the vomiting and diarrhoea. Remedies are administered to allay the sickness and diarrhoea and antibiotics are administered to arrest other side-effects of the virus. Early diagnosis is essential for the best chance of a full recovery, and intensive nursing is needed during the illness and convalescence. Puppies which contract the virus may have retarded growth and development, but future immunity is almost guaranteed. Vaccination is advised and is usually applied at the time of vaccination against the other major infectious diseases. Blood tests will reveal the level of immunity so that a preventative inoculation can be administered.

PROLONGED SOFT PALATE

Some Bernese experience breathing difficulties in situations of stress or activity caused by a reduced supply of oxygen. The soft palate acts as a flexible barrier between the pharynx and the mouth, and its enlargement, brought about by excessive vibration, will restrict the passage of air into the lungs so causing asphyxia. Surgical correction can succeed in reducing the risk of further incidence, but not all cases are operable. Only veterinary examination will confirm whether the diagnosis is in fact correct.

Dogs with a prolonged soft palate are prone to heatstroke, and it is not unknown for some stud dogs with the condition to reach a near-collapsed state during and after a mating due to the restriction of oxygen. The condition is not acquired; it is the way that the dog is made and the condition passes on to successive generations. Males seem more likely to have the condition, but this may be directly related to temperament, awareness of sexual stimulus and an increased likelihood of responding to stressful situations. Even after correction, those with the condition should not be bred from.

PYOMETRA

This is a condition affecting the reproduction tract of the bitch and is very common. It can affect both breeding bitches and those who have never known maternal duties – young and old alike. The most likely time for symptoms to be noticed is between four and eight weeks after a season and prompt veterinary action is needed. Two types of the condition occur –

open and closed. Open pyometra involves the loss of a thick reddish-brown putrid discharge from the bitch's vagina, accompanied by signs of abdominal enlargement, increased thirst, depression and shock. Closed pyometra cases lose no discharge, although any male dogs in the household may be attracted to the smell of the bitch. But because of the absorption of the fluid in the uterus into the bloodstream, the other symptoms as seen in the open form of the illness are more acute.

Spaying – removal of the ovaries and uterus – is often needed, although some cases will respond to medicines designed to contract the uterus and so flush out the accumulated fluid. Hormone imbalance seems to be the most likely cause, and so bitches treated medically are likely to experience the condition again after the next season. Progestogens given in treatment of mis-matings or to control the oestrus cycle can give rise to the condition, but some newer progestogens can reduce the risk enormously.

Umbilical Hernia

Many Bernese puppies have umbilical hernias and it is rare for these to cause any problems for the dogs. This type of hernia is formed at birth when the abdomen wall fails to heal over at the umbilicus. It is, in effect, a weakening where the ring of muscle fails to close so allowing a protrusion of fat to pass through and lie under the skin of the abdomen. It is noticed as a small, soft fluctuating swelling which causes no discomfort. Most hernias will have closed by the time puppies are about sixteen-weeks-old. Either the protrusion will remain outside the stomach wall but feel firm, or it may have retracted inside the abdomen. If the hernia can still be manipulated back into the abdomen after this age, then veterinary advice should be sought. Any umbilical hernia which is becoming visibly larger should be investigated without delay. It has been suggested that umbilical hernias are inherited.

Warts (Papilloma)

Often seen on Bernese of middle age and older, warts rarely give cause for concern or result in complications. They can appear on any area of the body, the most common being found around the eyelids and on the lips. Growth is usually slow, and they do not interfere with normal function unless they become damaged or reach gross size. Surgical removal is appropriate in some cases, other warts can be tied of with surgical thread and these will wither and fall away within days. Warts on the gums or inside the mouth can grow alarmingly fast and these should be carefully monitored to prevent interference with eating. Veterinary advice should be sought, if in doubt, as noticeable increase in size of any wart or growth could indicate serious underlying problems.